The Jewish People

BOOK THREE

By DEBORAH PESSIN

ILLUSTRATIONS BY RUTH LEVIN

UNITED SYNAGOGUE COMMISSION

THE JEWISH PEOPLE

Book Three

ON JEWISH EDUCATION · *NEW YORK · 1953–5713*

Fourth Printing, January, 1958

Copyright 1953 by The United Synagogue of America

All rights reserved. No part of this book may be reproduced in any form without permission in writing from the publisher except by a reviewer who may quote brief passages in a review to be printed in a magazine or newspaper. Design by Peter Oldenburg. Printed in the United States of America.

*To the Memory of
My Father
Rabbi Solomon Pessin*

PREFACE

WITH THIS VOLUME we complete the survey of the vast panorama of Jewish life. The writing of this history has been most gratifying to the author not only for the satisfaction of transmitting to children—the most impressionable and receptive of readers—the illustrious and heroic story of our people, but also for the enthusiasm with which the volumes of this history series have been received by the audience for whom they were written. Often, in the process of writing, the author has felt the illumination and warmth which are at the heart of Jewish life. She hopes that this experience has been reflected in the pages of these books.

The author has been fortunate for the interest of the many educators and rabbis who read the completed manuscripts. The manuscript of the third volume was read by Rabbi Michael Alper, Nathan Fish and Theresa K. Silber. The author wishes to thank them for their numerous suggestions for improving this volume. The members of the United Synagogue Commission on Jewish Education also read the manuscript. The author is particularly grateful to Hillel Henkin, Reuben Resnick and Dr. Samuel Sussman for their helpful suggestions. She also wishes to thank the members of the Committee on Textbook Publications, Henry R. Goldberg, Chairman of the Committee, Barnet Cohen, Rabbi George Ende, Dr. Solomon Grayzel, Rabbi Isidore S. Meyer, for their painstaking criticisms. Thanks are due also to Hillel Millgram who was kind enough to read the manuscript and offer suggestions for revision. The author is happy to thank Ruth Levin, the artist, who continued in the third volume the splendid illustrations she did for the first two volumes of *The Jewish People*.

It would take many words to express the deep gratitude the author feels toward Dr. Leo L. Honor, her consultant in the writing of all three volumes of *The Jewish People*. Dr. Honor has been more than a consultant. Not only his guidance, but his enthusiasm as well have often pointed up the direction and emphasis this history has taken.

It is equally difficult to convey the extent of the contribution of Dr. Abraham E. Millgram, Educational Director of the United Synagogue Commission on Jewish Education, in the preparation of this set of history books. Dr. Millgram was constantly at the author's side, giving unstintingly of his time, energy and Jewish learning. His many valuable suggestions as well as his encouragement eased the process of bringing this set of books to a successful completion.

DEBORAH PESSIN

CONTENTS

Dear Readers, 11

UNIT ONE

In Search of New Homes

CHAPTER 1. Welcome in Turkey	17
CHAPTER 2. In the Land of Memories	29
CHAPTER 3. Homes in Holland	39
CHAPTER 4. Homes in the New World	51

UNIT TWO

Light and Shadow in Poland

CHAPTER 1. A Day in Lublin	61
CHAPTER 2. A Nation of Students	78
CHAPTER 3. The False Messiah	89
CHAPTER 4. The Rise of Hasidism	99

UNIT THREE

Leaving the Ghettos

CHAPTER 1. Opening the Ghetto Gates	115
CHAPTER 2. Entering the Outside World	127
CHAPTER 3. Three Ways of Judaism	135

UNIT FOUR

In the Land of the Czars

CHAPTER 1. Oppression Under Czarism	147
CHAPTER 2. Enlightenment	160

CHAPTER 3. Auto-Emancipation 171
CHAPTER 4. Zionism 178

UNIT FIVE

In the Land of the Free

CHAPTER 1. The First Settlers 191
CHAPTER 2. New Builders of America 207
CHAPTER 3. Builders of Judaism 216
CHAPTER 4. Settlers From Eastern Europe 232
CHAPTER 5. The First World War 248

UNIT SIX

The Rebirth of Israel

CHAPTER 1. Pioneers in Palestine 259
CHAPTER 2. Between Two Wars 270
CHAPTER 3. Resistance and War 281
CHAPTER 4. Israel 294

Index, 307

Dear Readers:

HISTORY IS MORE than just a record of facts. When we hear mentioned the year 1492, for example, we naturally think of Columbus on the threshold of the New World. But behind Columbus, on the other side of the ocean over which he sailed, we see scientists making discoveries, navigators exploring new waters, restless minds reaching into unknown worlds. Behind Columbus stood the science of his day, the discoveries, the search for greater knowledge. If Columbus had not had these, he could never have made his memorable voyage.

And so it is with the facts in Jewish history. There was always a preparation for them, or they could not have taken place. One of the most amazing facts in Jewish history is this: The Jews were often conquered, exiled, and persecuted. Yet they continued to live on and on.

In the first two volumes of *The Jewish People* we tried to explain the "preparation" for this astonishing fact in the history of the Jews and of mankind. We learned, in Book One, how the Jews first entered Palestine as a nation, bringing with them memories of their patriarchs, who worshipped one God, and of their great liberator Moses, who led them out of slavery and gave them the Ten Commandments. These memories were the bonds that united them, and when the bonds weakened, that is, when the Jews began to forget their past, teachers and leaders fortunately arose to bring the past before them again.

As the years went by, misfortunes often came upon the Jewish people in the little land of Palestine. There came a time when the nation split into two kingdoms, the kingdom of Israel and the kingdom of Judea. The ten tribes of Israel were conquered and exiled by the king of Assyria. Living in a strange land, most of them let themselves forget their past. They learned to worship the gods of their conquerors, and they vanished, in time, among the people with whom they lived.

Years later, Judea was conquered by the armies of Babylonia and thousands of Judeans were exiled to Babylonia. But by this time the teachings of the prophets had taken deep root, and there were many Judeans who did not permit themselves to forget their past. They insisted on worshipping one God, though the people about them worshipped many gods. They insisted on keeping their own customs and their own way of life. Eventually, Babylonia was conquered by Cyrus, who gave the Judeans, or the Jews, permission to return to Judea. Many Jews then returned to Judea to rebuild their land and their life as a nation.

In Book Two of the *The Jewish People* we learned how the Jews continued to be true to their own way of life, to their religion, their customs, and to the teachings of the prophets. Great teachers arose to make this way of life stronger than ever. The Jews were conquered by stronger nations time and again, but they continued to live as Jews. All the terror and persecution Antiochus brought upon the little nation could not destroy it. Nor could the mighty Roman armies destroy the Jewish people. When the Jews scattered over the face of the earth, their memories and their loyalties went with them. They continued to study the Torah and the Talmud, which became a part of their daily lives. They built schools and academies, so that they could hand on to their children what they had inherited from the past—their religion, their customs, their festivals, their laws, their great literature. Unlike other people who were conquered and exiled, they did not disappear, because their own way of life continued from one generation to the next.

The fact that the Jews continued to live their own way of life does not mean that they did not enter into the life about them. The Jews helped develop the civilization of whatever land they settled in. They gave the world the Bible and the idea of one God. They helped develop science, industry, crafts, commerce. Often they taught their neighbors the skills and crafts they had brought with them from the East.

Despite their gifts to the world, however, the Jews were often persecuted. As Christianity spread, many of the early Christian leaders wanted everyone to accept the teachings of Christianity. The Jews, refusing to abandon their own religion, found themselves discriminated against and often, cruelly persecuted.

While the Jews lived under Mohammedan rule in Spain, they enjoyed complete freedom. But when Spain was conquered by Christian rulers their freedom began gradually to disappear. To escape persecution, many Jews outwardly accepted Christianity, but in secret they remained loyal to their own religion. These secret Jews, who were called Marranos, were often discovered observing the Jewish customs. To discourage and punish loyalty to Judaism among the Marranos, the Inquisition was set up. Thousands of Marranos, found "guilty," by the judges of the Inquisition, of loyalty to Judaism, were imprisoned, tortured, and often burned at the *auto-da-fé*.

Torquemado, the master of the Inquisition, finally concluded that as long as there were Jews in Spain who openly practiced Judaism, the Marranos would always look to them as an example to follow. So Torquemado, who wanted all of Spain to be Christian, persuaded Isabella and Ferdinand, the rulers of Spain, to expel the Jews from the land.

This volume, the third of *The Jewish People*, continues the story of the Jews from their exile from Spain to the present day. In this book we shall learn how they fared in many lands, in Holland, Turkey, Poland, Russia, in the Germanic lands, and in the great New World of America. And finally, we shall read about the miracle of modern Israel—how the dreams and the patience of many thousands of Jews were rewarded at last when Israel was reborn in its ancient homeland.

UNIT ONE

In Search of New Homes

THE YEAR 1492 was an important year for those who were oppressed in the Old World. In that year Columbus opened the route to a world that was free, the route to America.

With other pioneers, Jews crossed the perilous sea to make homes in America. But whether they migrated to the New World or remained in the Old World, they went to those places or lands that offered them freedom. And wherever they went, they helped build civilization, and greater freedom, and the rights of man.

CHAPTER ONE

Welcome in Turkey

On the Ninth Day of Ab

On the ninth day of Ab, in the year 586 B.C.E., the Temple in Jerusalem was destroyed by the armies of Babylonia.

It was also on the ninth day of Ab, in the year 70, that the second Temple was destroyed, this time by the legions of Rome.

And it was on the ninth day of Ab, in the year 1492, that the Jews were expelled from Spain.

Wherever the news reached, in the widespread towns and cities of the world, the Jews again bowed their heads and mourned because of the tragedy that had swept over them.

Spain was the one land in Europe where the Jews had lived in freedom. Here they had made their homes for more than a thousand years, helping to bring it from barbarism to civilization. Under the rule of the Mohammedans, they had risen to greater and greater glory. Their doctors had attended the sick. Their statesmen had been advisers to the rulers. Their scholars and poets had written books and songs. Their scientists had advanced the knowledge of their day. Their merchants had brought silks and spices and tapestries and rugs from the East. Their artisans had made cloth and leather goods, implements and ornaments. Their farmers had cultivated orchards and vineyards. Their rabbis had spread the knowledge of the Torah. While Jews had been expelled from other lands, or driven from one city to another, in Spain they had moved through all the land in freedom.

But Spain was conquered at last by Christian rulers. Then, bit by bit, the Jews were deprived of their freedom. In 1492 came the final blow. The Jews were expelled from Spain. Numbed with grief and despair, they were thrust out of the land they had helped to build.

Seeking New Homes

Finding new homes was not easy. England and France had expelled the Jews. In the Germanic lands, which were made up of many states, they were hounded into ghettos and forced to wear badges to distinguish them from their neighbors. Whenever a ruler pleased, he could order them to leave his kingdom or pay for the privilege of remaining. The Germanic lands could therefore be no refuge for the Jews who were driven from Spain.

Most of the refugees went to Portugal, for Portugal was nearest to Spain, and the Jews had only to cross the border. Jews who had managed to take their money out of Spain were welcomed by the king of Portugal, for money meant more income for the king's treasury and greater prosperity for the land. But like Spain, Portugal too had set up the Inquisition. Four years later, in 1496, the Jews were expelled from Portugal, and again they were forced to seek new homes.

They sometimes found homes in the cities of Italy, or in other lands bordering the Mediterranean Sea. But there were many Jews who left Spain who never found homes at all. They were robbed by the captains of the vessels on which they sailed, then thrown into the sea, or left to die on desert islands. Some were abandoned on the shores of Africa, where they died of pestilence or hunger. Thousands were sold into slavery after being robbed by the captains of the vessels which were to bring them to safety. But of these, many were ransomed by their people. It is told that the sons of a rich Jewish family in Pisa, Italy, practically made their homes on the quay of the city. Eagerly they awaited the ships sailing into dock, so that they could welcome and ransom their enslaved brothers.

Back to the East

As the Jews had once drifted from their homeland in the East, because of exile, hunger or oppression, many now returned to the East, to the region of the earth where their forefathers had lived. But now it was to a new empire they went, to the empire of the Ottomans, or Turks, which stretched over many lands. Out of Asia, a group of tribes known as Turks had come, and they had seized many lands from the Christian rulers. They had swept over Syria, Egypt, Palestine, Mesopotamia, and over the countries of southeastern Europe.

Welcome in Turkey

Even before the year 1492 Jews had drifted into the lands ruled by the Turks. After 1492, the year when King Ferdinand issued the decree that all Jews must leave Spain, they came in increasing numbers. From Spain, from Portugal, from other lands of oppression, they fled to the empire of the friendly Turkish sultans.

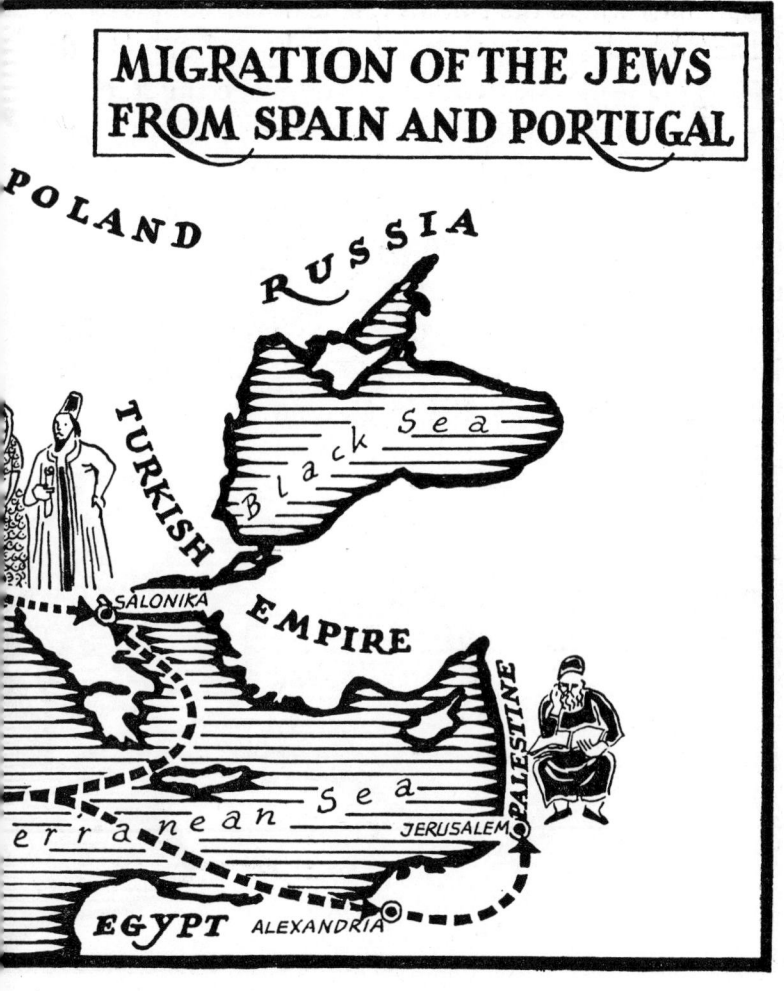

Settling in Turkey

The Jews who came to Turkey brought with them their skills and their knowledge. For these things the rulers of Spain could not take from them. And those who were rich and were able to bring their wealth, brought this too to the lands where the sultans reigned.

The Turks were a simple, agricultural people, unskilled in many of the industries which had developed in Europe. The Jews helped develop commerce and industry and handicrafts. Their doctors healed the sick and their statesmen became advisers to the sultans. They opened bazaars and stores, and they brought printing presses into the backward country. And this, the French ambassador reported to the king of France, was a wonderful thing for the Turks. For now the Turks could have books printed in Latin, Greek, Italian, Hebrew.

JEWS IN TURKEY

The freedom the Jews had once enjoyed in Spain, under Mohammedan rulers, was now restored to them in Turkey, which was also under Mohammedan rule. Jewish life became rich and strong. Academies were opened for the study of the Talmud. Constantinople and Salonika became, in the sixteenth century, the largest Jewish centers in the world.

Gracia Mendes

There lived, in the land of Portugal, a rich and beautiful Marrano woman whose name was Gracia Mendes. When Gracia's husband, who was a banker, died, she decided to go to a land where she could worship as she pleased. But she wanted to go to Antwerp first, where there was an important branch of her family's firm. Accompanied by her daughter Reyna, by her handsome nephew, Joseph Nasi, and by other members of her family, she came to Antwerp to settle her financial affairs. Antwerp, a Dutch city, was then ruled by the king of Spain, and Gracia and her family still had to pretend they were Christians.

Gracia's daughter, Reyna, was soon sought in marriage by many wealthy noblemen. But when Reyna rejected every suitor, rumors began to spread that the beautiful girl might be Jewish and would marry only a man of her own faith. Joseph, too, began to attract attention. The handsome Marrano, who moved freely about in the king's court, was envied by many noblemen who would have liked to see his downfall.

When Gracia felt that it was no longer safe to live in Antwerp, she fled to Venice, Reyna and Joseph again accompanying her. In Venice, however, Gracia was betrayed, and she was imprisoned on the charge of trying to abandon Christianity. The government of Venice seized Gracia's possessions, and the king of France, who was indebted to her banking firm, declared that he would not repay his debt.

Joseph Nasi managed to get out of Venice and reach Turkey. Helped by Jewish friends at court, he quickly won the sympathy of the sultan, Suleiman, who was feared by the government of Venice. When Suleiman announced that Gracia Mendes was under his protection, she was freed at once and her property was restored. Gracia was at last able to come to Turkey, where she could live openly as a Jewess.

Favorite of the Sultan

Joseph Nasi, who married his cousin Reyna, lived like a prince in Turkey. For not only was Joseph Nasi a wealthy man, but he soon became the favorite of the sultan, Suleiman. Like his aunt Gracia, who used her wealth to help Jews escape from Spain and Portugal, Joseph, too, helped them find homes in friendly lands.

Joseph had lived in many lands, and his wealth had opened the doors of courts and council chambers. Experience had taught him the art of diplomacy, the ways of dealing with ambassadors from foreign countries. The sultan therefore found Joseph a valuable adviser, and Joseph rose higher and higher in his favor, till he became the most powerful man at court. When Suleiman died and his son Selim II came to the throne, Joseph served him as faithfully as he had served his father.

In gratitude for Joseph's services, Selim bestowed many gifts and honors upon his favorite. He made him Duke of Naxos, and appointed him a member of the guard of honor. So powerful did Joseph become, that ambassadors of foreign lands often asked him to speak to the sultan in their behalf.

But it was from Selim's father, Suleiman, that Joseph received his most valuable gift. This gift was the city of Tiberias, in Palestine, and Joseph hoped to make it a refuge for the Jews.

PILGRIMS DISEMBARKING IN PALESTINE

AFTER CONTEMPORARY WOODCUT

Joseph's Dream

Palestine, at this time, was a poor, neglected land. It had been torn by years of war. It had been a battleground for Christian crusaders and Mohammedans, each claiming that the Holy Land was theirs. The Christians claimed it because Jesus had been born there, and the Mohammedans claimed it because, they said, Mohammed had ascended to heaven from Mount Zion. The struggle had been carried on through many centuries, till there was only poverty in the land, and barren fields and empty cities. The few Jews who still lived there were poor tailors, cobblers, dyers, weavers, and they looked to their people in other lands for support.

Tiberias, like the rest of the land, was poor. To make it a prosperous city, and to develop the regions around it, Joseph Nasi planned to introduce an important industry, the manufacture of silk. Silk was usually brought from distant India, often at great risk, for pirate ships roamed the seas. If silk could be manufactured in Ti-

TIBERIAS

berias, it could then be brought to European markets at less cost and with less danger. In addition, Tiberias could be made into a thriving, prosperous community, and a home for many Jews.

To carry out his plans, Joseph rebuilt the walls of Tiberias and had mulberry trees planted, so that the silkworm could be cultivated. He then sent out a call to the Jews to come to Tiberias, providing ships to bring them there.

But Joseph's plans were in vain. War broke out between Turkey and Venice, and Joseph was unable to send his ships to Italy. A few Marranos did manage to leave Italy, but they were seized by pirates and sold as slaves.

The settlement of the Jews in their Holy Land, however, did not end with Joseph's dream. For the dream was not Joseph's alone. It was the dream of many Jews to return to the land which they called *Eretz Yisrael*, the Land of Israel. And though Palestine was poor, it drew many Jews who wanted to find rest in the land of their fathers.

For the Pupil

THINGS TO READ:

1. Kalischer, Betty, *Watchmen of the Night*, "A Place of Refuge," page 108.
2. Lurie, Rose, *The Great March, Book Two*, "Hail the Duke!" page 46.
3. Pessin, Deborah, *Giants on the Earth*, "The French Ambassador Takes a Walk," page 9.

THINGS TO TALK ABOUT:
1. How had the Jews helped develop the civilization of Spain?
2. How did they help advance the civilization of Turkey?
3. Why did the Jews open schools and academies wherever they went?

THINGS TO DO:
1. Trace, on a map, the route the Jews might have taken from Spain to Portugal, from Spain to Turkey, from Spain to Africa.
2. Write the story of a child who sails with his parents from Spain and finally makes his home in Turkey.

⋘ *Teacher's Bibliography*

Grayzel, Solomon, *A History of the Jews,* Jewish Publication Society, 1947, pp. 416-437; 460-464.

Learsi, Rufus, *Israel,* World Publishing Co., 1949, pp. 313-334.

Margolis and Marx, *History of the Jewish People,* Jewish Publication Society, 1927, pp. 470-476; 512-517.

Roth, Cecil, *A History of the Marranos,* Jewish Publication Society, 1932.

CHAPTER TWO

In the Land of Memories

The Holy Land

The Jews who came to Palestine from Spain and Portugal knew that they would not find riches in the land of their fathers, or bustling towns and great academies. They wanted only to live in the land that had cradled them when they were a young nation. They wanted the land of their patriarchs, Abraham, Isaac and Jacob, the land of David and Solomon, the land of their prophets. They wanted their holy cities, filled with memories of the past.

Holy Cities of the Holy Land

Holiest of all cities, to the Jews, were the cities of Hebron, Jerusalem and Tiberias. Hebron was the city where the patriarchs were buried. In Jerusalem, holiest of the holy cities, Solomon had built the Temple. Tiberias, in Galilee, had been the home of the scholars who helped develop the Palestinian Talmud.

Soon another city was to become a holy city. This city was Safed, which nestled in the hills of Galilee.

In the Hills of Galilee

Safed had never been important in Jewish history. Never was it mentioned in the Bible, and only rarely in the literature of the rabbis. Wars had passed it by, for it was but a small town, and few people lived there. When the wars were over, Safed was still there, peaceful and isolated as it had always been. But now and then people climbed the hills to reach it and make their homes there.

Slowly it grew. Men tilled the fields around Safed and led a simple life. They drew water at the town well and carried it home on their shoulders. They shopped in the marketplaces for vegetables, flour and oil. They kept small stores, or wove cloth, or made utensils for the homes of Safed.

SAFED TODAY

As the Jews began to migrate into the empire of the sultan, some of them came to Palestine, which was under the sultan's rule. Then Safed, like Jerusalem, gained many new settlers.

Men who were interested in studying the Torah and the Talmud came to Safed, where they could lead a quiet life. By the sixteenth century, Safed had eighteen academies where the Talmud was taught. With its many schools and synagogues and scholars, Safed became an important Jewish center of learning.

Kabbalah

Many of the new settlers in Safed had come from Spain and Portugal. They had suffered oppression and exile, and they had seen the horrors of the Inquisition. It was not strange, then, that their minds fled from the world where they had known sorrow and grief, and dwelt in a world of wonderful things to come. This had happened in the past, when Rome was master of Judea. Then, too, people had thought of better days, and had dreamed of the Messiah, who would bring peace and justice to mankind.

So it was now in Safed, among those who had fled or who had been exiled from Spain and Portugal. When will the suffering of Israel end? they asked themselves. When will the Messiah come? How does God rule the world? What must we do to be worthy of the coming of the Messiah?

To help themselves find the answers to the questions that troubled them, they studied mystical books. One of the most famous of these books was the *Zohar,* which means light. The *Zohar,* many people believed, had been written by Rabbi Simeon ben Yoḥai, one of the great teachers who had lived in Judea during the second century. So important did the mystics consider the *Zohar,* that they ranked it second to the Bible.

Through the *Zohar,* the mystics hoped that the secrets of the Bible would be revealed to them. For they believed that the answers to their questions must be in the Bible, since the Bible was the word of God. Yet, if they read the Bible, word by word, sentence by sentence, they could not find the hidden messages which they believed the Bible contained. They could find only the simple messages, which any reader could find. But what they sought was God's secret message.

Then it must be, the mystics believed, that behind the simple message there was a deeper one which God had hidden from the eyes of the ordinary reader. But who could find the message? And how? What key could they use to unlock the mystery?

The key, they believed, was the *Zohar.* For the *Zohar* contained a commentary on the Bible. Not everyone, however, could read the *Zohar,* since it was written in a secret language. Only a handful of pious men could read it. They had received the secret of how to read the *Zohar* from other pious and worthy men.

We call the *Zohar* and other mystical writings *Kabbalah,* which means received, or handed down. And the students of the *Kabbalah* we call *Kabbalists.*

In their eagerness to find the secret message of God, the *Kabbalists* spent their days and nights studying the

Zohar and the Bible. Through their studies, their prayers and the pious lives they led, they hoped they would become worthy of learning God's will.

Safed became the center for the study of the *Kabbalah*. As bees drawn to honey, *Kabbalists* were drawn to Safed from all parts of the world.

Then came a man called Isaac Luria, the most famous of all the students of the *Kabbalah*. From the time of Isaac Luria, Safed, like Hebron, Jerusalem and Tiberias, became known as a holy city.

The Lion and His Whelps

Isaac Luria's parents were born in Germany, but they had migrated to Jerusalem when he was a young child. When Isaac's father died, his mother took her family to Cairo, in Egypt, where her brother, who was a wealthy man, could help her.

Isaac, in time, became a rabbi. Like many men of his day, he also became a student of the *Kabbalah*. The young rabbi wanted to devote all his time to the *Kab-*

balah. He wanted to live a holy, pious life, away from the hurly-burly of the world about him. So he built himself a humble hut on the bank of the Nile River. Here he lived alone, returning to his family in Cairo only for the Sabbath.

Often, as he sat studying in his lonely hut, he believed that he spoke with the prophet Elijah. Legend tells us that Luria received a message bidding him leave Egypt and go to Safed. With his wife and child, Luria went to the city in the hills of Galilee, and there he became the leader of a group of *Kabbalists*.

With their families, the followers of Luria formed their own small community in dwellings built around a common courtyard, so that they could always be together. Luria taught his disciples the *Zohar,* and how to live according to what he believed was the will of God. Not satisfied with merely learning God's message, Luria and his followers wanted to hasten the coming of the Messiah. To do this, they lived lives of extreme piety. They believed they must think certain thoughts and feel great joy while praying. All their thoughts, all their actions, all their studies, had one purpose, to bring the Messiah.

So great was Luria's influence on the people of Safed, that they called him "the holy man," "the Divine *Kabbalist.*" His followers called him ARI, or lion, using the initials of the words *A*shkenazi *R*abbi *I*saac, Rabbi Isaac of Germany. And his followers were known as the "lion's whelps."

Luria died when he was thirty-eight years old, but the "lion's whelps" carried on his teachings, bringing them to many lands.

KABBALISTIC AMULETS

A Prepared Table

Another great name that has come down to us from Safed is that of Joseph Karo. Karo too was a *Kabbalist*. It is not for this, however, that he is famous, but for a book he wrote, the *Shulḥan Arukh* (Prepared Table). The *Shulḥan Arukh*, a collection of every Jewish law up to the time that the book was written, told its readers what religious laws they were to follow from the moment they arose in the morning to the moment they went to sleep.

It told them how to pray, how to wash, how to eat, how they were to prepare their food, how their clothes were to be made, how the festivals were to be observed, how the poor were to be cared for, how business was to be carried on. Every law was simply stated and set before the reader, like food on a table.

Strangely enough, Joseph Karo did not consider the *Shulḥan Arukh* his most important work. It was another work, to which he devoted thirty years, that he considered his life's work. *Beth Joseph* (House of Joseph) was a four volume work, a vast collection of the Jewish laws, while the *Shulḥan Arukh* was merely a summary of *Beth Joseph*. Yet Karo is scarcely remembered for the work to which he gave so many years of his life. It is the *Shulḥan Arukh* which became important. To this day, it is the daily guide for many Jews all over the world.

The man who could discipline himself for years in the task of collecting and arranging thousands of laws, was also a man who could let his fancy roam. Like Luria, Karo too had visions. It seemed to him that an angel spoke to him, and the voice of the angel was like the voice of a mother, urging him on in his work, reproaching him when he slept too much, pleading with him to study the *Kabbalah* more diligently. It was his angel, his teacher, who bade him go to Safed, where he could live a holy life.

Like Isaac Luria, Joseph Karo expressed the spirit of his day. Both men, uprooted from the lands where they were born, found peace in the land of their fathers. And in the holy city of Safed, they studied the *Kabbalah*, dreaming of justice and freedom for their people.

∿∿ For the Pupil

THINGS TO TALK ABOUT:

1. Why was Palestine the Holy Land for Jews, Christians and Mohammedans?
2. Why did many Jews turn to the *Kabbalah* for comfort?
3. Why did they dream about the Messiah?

THINGS TO DO:

1. For the Jews scattered in many lands, Palestine had numerous associations. When they thought of Palestine they thought of its holy cities, of David, Solomon, Elijah, the prophets, the Temple. Can you write a little story or essay about Palestine as the "Land of Memories"?
2. Make an animated map of the "Land of Memories."

∿∿ Teacher's Bibliography

Grayzel, Solomon, *A History of the Jews*, pp. 464-472.

Margolis and Marx, *History of the Jewish People*, pp. 518-524.

Myers, Jack, *The Story of the Jewish People*, volume III, Bloch Publishing Co., 1925, pp. 1-57.

Schechter, Solomon, *Studies in Judaism*, Second Series, Jewish Publication Society, 1908, "Safed in the Sixteenth Century," pp. 202-285.

AMULETS

CHAPTER THREE

ᴡᴡ Homes in Holland

An Incident in Amsterdam

One day in October, about a century after the expulsion from Spain, a group of armed men came walking briskly down a street in Amsterdam. They stopped before a house with drawn curtains and barred windows. For several moments they stood listening, but no sound came from the silent house. They heard only the faintest whisper, which might have been the bough of a tree scraping against the shingled roof.

As a crowd of men and women gathered to watch, one of the policemen banged upon the door of the house with his fist. "Open up in the name of the law!" he cried. But there was no sound from the house, only a deeper silence. A second policeman stepped forward and set his shoulder against the door. With a mighty heave, he burst open the door, and the armed men entered the house.

Minutes went by as the crowd of people in the street grew larger. At last the policemen emerged, escorting two pale, terrified men. The crowd continued to watch curiously as the policemen and their two prisoners disappeared down the street and into the courthouse. The curtains on one of the windows was suddenly pushed aside and a face peered out for a moment. Then the curtains fell back into place and the face vanished.

In the courthouse, the magistrate sat listening gravely to the two prisoners who had been brought before him. They spoke to him rapidly, with a strange pleading in their voices. But in the eyes of the magistrate there was no understanding of what they spoke, only a growing bewilderment. Suddenly a man entered through a doorway at the back of the room. He approached the judge, signing to the prisoners to be silent. The newcomer could not speak Dutch either. He spoke in Latin, hoping that the magistrate, who was a learned man, would understand him.

The prisoners, he explained, were his friends, refugees from Portugal, and they were still unable to speak the language of the Dutch people. They were Marranos, secret Jews who had come to Holland to escape the Inquisition. He too was a Jew, and his name was Jacob Tirado. He and his friends had been conducting their Yom Kippur services when the police had broken into the house.

Light broke in the eyes of the judge. It was all a mistake, he explained, and now he understood why they prayed in secret. He had received complaints from a number of people that there was a group of Catholics in the house with the drawn curtains and the barred windows. They had caught a glimpse of men praying, and they thought the prayer shawls were a disguise of some kind. Since the Netherlands had thrown off the yoke of Catholic Spain and had become Protestant, they wanted no more Catholics or Inquisitors in their land. The Jews, said the magistrate, were unfamiliar to the people of Amsterdam, and so the mistake had been made.

Then Jacob Tirado spoke again. The Netherlands could gain much by letting the Jews come in freely, he said. The Jews were industrious and loyal, and they were skilled in many things. Some of the Jews were wealthy. The people of the Netherlands had a fine merchant fleet. With the loyalty and wealth of the Marranos, trade with foreign lands could be improved, and all of the Netherlands would thus benefit.

The magistrate nodded his agreement. Abruptly, he dismissed the prisoners. The three Jews left the court and returned to the silent house where their friends awaited them to continue their Yom Kippur services.

Two years later, in the city of Amsterdam, the first synagogue on the soil of Holland was opened. And the Jews of Amsterdam, who had grown from ten families

THE SPANISH AND PORTUGUESE SYNAGOGUE, AMSTERDAM, 1675

to four hundred families, dressed in their holiday clothes and hastened with joy to their new house of prayer.

On the Street of the Jews

About fifty years passed since the first synagogue opened in Amsterdam. In a house on *Joden Bree Straat*, which was the street of the Jews in Amsterdam, a man stood at a window looking out. The man's name was Rembrandt and he was a famous Dutch painter. Rembrandt had chosen to make his home on *Joden Bree Straat* because he liked the beauty of the people who lived there. There were Jews throughout Amsterdam, for they were permitted to live wherever they pleased. But because people who come from the same land often prefer to live together, many of the Jews who came to Amsterdam had made their homes on the same street.

Rembrandt's eye quickened with pleasure as he saw a woman, followed by a servant, returning from the market. The woman was tall and queenly, and her dark eyes, under the white lace of her starched cap, were the blackest jet. And there, not far behind her, was a man whose face brought visions of the prophets. Rembrandt sighed. He could not paint all the Jews on *Joden Bree Straat*. But he was glad that his neighbor and friend, Rabbi Manasseh ben Israel, had consented to have his portrait painted. Rabbi Manasseh ben Israel was a busy man, with the many books he wrote, the Hebrew printing press he had set up, the wide correspondence he carried on, even with Queen Christina of Sweden, who delighted in the Dutch rabbi's scholarship and wisdom.

Rembrandt turned away from the window of his house at No. 2 *Joden Bree Straat* and went to prepare his paints and brushes. Manasseh ben Israel, who lived at No. 19, would be coming in soon to have his portrait finished before he set out for England.

Manasseh ben Israel

Manasseh ben Israel loved his home in Holland. Since the brave little country, under the leadership of William of Orange, had thrown off the yoke of Spain, his people had found a new place of refuge. William of Orange had established religious freedom in Holland, and so many

Jews had come there. Not only Jews fleeing the Inquisition, like Manasseh ben Israel's own father, had come to Holland. There were Jews from Germany, Italy, and even from distant Poland.

But it was impossible for all the Jews to go to Holland, or to Turkey, or even to the Holy Land. Manasseh ben Israel wanted other countries as well to open their doors to his people. There was England, which had expelled the Jews in the thirteenth century. More than three hundred years had passed since the expulsion. Tyrant kings in England had been overthrown. Oliver Cromwell, who was the head of the Puritan party, now headed the government of England. Cromwell loved the Bible and the Jewish heroes of the past. Did not Cromwell turn to the Bible for guidance? And did he not like to speak of himself as Judah Maccabee? Surely, thought Manasseh ben Israel, he would consent to let the Jews enter England.

The Dutch rabbi, who studied the *Kabbalah*, believed that the Messiah would come only when the Ten Lost Tribes were found, and when the Jews were scattered throughout the world. Nothing was known of the Ten Lost Tribes of Israel, who had been exiled from Palestine more than two thousand years back by the king of Assyria. But Manasseh ben Israel believed that the Indians in America were the Ten Lost Tribes. All that remained, the rabbi believed, was to have the Jews scattered throughout the world. This could not be done, however, if England did not permit them to dwell upon her soil.

Manasseh ben Israel therefore sailed for England to persuade Cromwell and Parliament to permit the Jews to enter. The Dutch rabbi was received with great honors in London. And when he addressed Parliament, he asked for justice for his people. He spoke of the abilities of the Jews, and of how they helped enrich whatever land they dwelt in.

Cromwell was friendly both to the Dutch rabbi and to the Jews, and he too asked for their return. But there were many members of the clergy who objected to having Jews in England. And there were many merchants who feared the rivalry of Jewish merchants.

Manasseh ben Israel sailed at last for home, his plea denied. Yet he did not fail. He had stirred up the country, till every man took sides. And in the end it was justice that won in freedom-loving England. In the year 1657, the very year the Dutch rabbi died, Jews were permitted to live in London. And gradually, all of England was open to the Jews.

MANASSEH BEN ISRAEL
after an etching by Rembrandt

The Gentle Grinder of Lenses

In the village of Rijnsburg, in Holland, there is a street called *Spinoza Laan*. In the shade of tall ash trees on *Spinoza Laan* stands a little house. Many people come to see the house, as tourists come to see the homes of famous people.

But there is not much one can see in the house under the ash trees. A desk, a chair, a bookcase filled with books, many of them Hebrew, a pen, an inkwell, a sandpot, which was used for drying ink on a written page. The little house has a workshop. In it is an optician's lathe, a chimney, bellows. On the wall of this room is an inscription in Latin: "Do good and rejoice."

Though there is not much to see in the house on *Spinoza Laan*, there are always people who come to see it. For in this house, in the middle of the seventeenth century, lived the man Spinoza.

Spinoza's parents had come to Amsterdam from Spain, and when a child was born to them, they called him Baruch, which means blessed. Like all Jewish boys of his day, Baruch studied the Bible, the Talmud, the writings of the rabbis. But his eager young mind never seemed satisfied. He studied the Jewish philosophers, particularly Maimonides, the philosophers of the French, the writings of the Greeks and Romans, physics, mathematics, medicine, astronomy. But Spinoza's hunger was not only for books. In whatever books he read, he looked for the meaning of God, and of the world about him.

Spinoza wanted to find the meaning of God in his own

way, through the searchings of his own mind. And so he refused to follow some of the teachings of the rabbis which had been handed down through the ages. The Jews of Amsterdam had expected young Baruch to become a great rabbi among them. Now, they feared, he would become dangerous. For if he denied God, he might influence other Jewish youths to do the same. And worse still, all the Jews might be accused of being a godless people. Having suffered for the freedom to worship their God, they feared that now, through Baruch, they would lose that freedom. So the rabbis of Amsterdam excommunicated Baruch Spinoza, saying that he was no longer a member of the Jewish community.

But Spinoza was not troubled by the excommunication. He left the busy city of Amsterdam and went to live in its outskirts. He lived quietly, grinding lenses to make a living, while his thoughts were kept occupied with the conduct of man and the meaning of God.

Men interested in philosophy found their way to Spinoza's house, to hear his wisdom. Gradually, his fame as a philosopher spread beyond Holland, into other lands.

"When I was in Holland," a Frenchman once said when he returned to Paris, "I found a new fashion. It was fashionable to know Spinoza."

Though Spinoza was invited to the University of Heidelberg to be a professor of philosophy, he preferred to grind lenses, so that his mind would remain free. He lived humbly and quietly, interested only in the ideas that filled his mind.

As time passed, the fine powdered glass of the lenses Spinoza ground crept into his lungs. Still he worked on

SPINOZA AND HIS WORKROOM AT RHIJNSBURG

with his hands, so that his mind would be free. On and on he worked, his body wracked with coughing. And when his lungs could stand no more, Spinoza, one of the greatest philosophers the world has known, died quietly in his little house in Holland.

In a drawer of his desk his friends found his most famous work. It was a book called *Ethics,* and in it were the ideas that had occupied him while he was grinding lenses. All the world, he said, is God, the things about us and the thoughts within us. The man who was thought to be godless believed that all wisdom and all happiness are in the knowledge of God.

For the Pupil

THINGS TO READ:

1. Levinger, Elma, *Great Jews Since Bible Times*, "The Jews Come Back to England," page 96, and "The Man Who Made Spectacles," page 100.
2. Lurie, Rose, *The Great March*, "Never Give Up," page 19.
3. Pessin, Deborah, *Giants on the Earth*, "Open the Gates," page 20, and "The Maker of Spectacles," page 36.

THINGS TO TALK ABOUT:

1. Why did many people, fighting against tyranny, like those in Cromwell's day, turn to the Bible for guidance?
2. Can you think of instances in American history, where people longing or struggling for freedom turned to the Bible for inspiration? List the Negro spirituals you know. Which of them have Biblical references? Discuss the ideas in the spirituals.

THINGS TO DO:

Dramatize the story of how the Marranos were discovered in New Amsterdam, or dramatize one of the stories listed under THINGS TO READ.

Teacher's Bibliography

Grayzel, Solomon, *A History of the Jews*, pp. 490-499.

Learsi, Rufus, *Israel*, pp. 339-345.

Margolis and Marx, *History of the Jewish People*, pp. 486-500.

Zangwill, Israel, *Dreamers of the Ghetto*, Jewish Publication Society, 1898, "The Maker of Lenses," p. 186 ff.

CHAPTER FOUR

Homes in the New World

Renaissance

During the fourteenth, the fifteenth and the sixteenth centuries, a new spirit stirred through Europe. It began in Italy, and like a fresh wind, it blew over Germany, France, Holland, England. The new spirit was called Renaissance, which means rebirth, or, awakening. For there was born, in many men, the desire to be free of the narrow, cramping life of the Middle Ages.

People were beginning to tire of their bonds. They rediscovered old books filled with wisdom, the books of the Greeks and the Romans. And they found new beauties and truths in these books which had been closed to them.

As men let their thoughts roam, they began to think more boldly. People had once thought that the earth was the center of the universe. But Copernicus declared that the earth was only a planet in a vast system of planets, of which the sun was the center. People had believed that the earth was stationary. But Galileo said, the world moves!

As men began to reach out, they longed for greater freedom. Little Holland rose in arms and threw off the oppression of Spain. Men often revolted against the

Church. The movement called Protestantism was born. Wider and wider opened the horizons of the world. New discoveries were made. New instruments were invented. New routes were discovered to old lands. After the voyage of Columbus, new lands were explored beyond the Atlantic Ocean.

Jews helped spread the spirit of the Renaissance. The gift of the Bible to the world was theirs. They translated some of the books of the Arabs, the Romans, the Greeks. They taught Hebrew to students who wished to understand the language of the Bible. They helped develop science. They sailed to the new lands beyond the Atlantic Ocean. They hoped that they would find, in the new lands, the freedom they had lost in the Old World.

To the New World

The first lands to stake their claims in the New World were Spain and Portugal. In the sixteenth century, they sent soldiers and settlers to take and hold the lands in the west.

With each ship that returned to Europe, there came stories of the wonderful riches to be found in the fresh, green lands across the ocean—treasures hidden in forests and caves, silver mines deep in the earth, cities of marble gleaming on mountainsides.

The rulers of Spain and Portugal wanted the treasures of the New World, the gold and the silver and the precious stones. They also wanted the power that comes with ruling many lands. So they sent larger fleets and more settlers. Some people came because of greed. Some came because they were tired of the old life in Europe. Some, like most of the Jews who came, wanted freedom.

Each ship bringing soldiers and settlers to the western hemisphere also brought priests. They came to convert the Indians to Christianity and to keep an eye on the Marranos. The Inquisition was introduced into the New World, and as still happened in Spain and Portugal, Marranos caught practicing their Jewish customs were burned at the stake.

Still Jews continued to come. In Spain and Portugal

they had lived in crowded cities, house bordering house, so that each man knew what his neighbor was doing. But the New World seemed to stretch endlessly, with great wide spaces and virgin forestland. Perhaps, they thought, they could somehow escape the long, iron hand of the Inquisition.

Some of the new Jewish settlers lived in Mexico, which had been claimed by Spain, and in Brazil, which was under Portuguese rule. The Jews helped clear the forests and they planted sugar. They set up sugar mills and exported precious cargoes of sugar, importing goods needed by the settlers. And behind the closed doors of the houses they built on their wide plantations, they observed the customs of their fathers.

The Coming of the Dutch

Holland too wanted a share of the New World. So the Dutch West Indies Company, which was a company of Dutch merchants, sent a fleet across the Atlantic Ocean. In the year 1630, the Dutch captured from the Portuguese a part of Brazil and its chief city, Recife.

With Dutch rule, freedom came for the Jewish settlers. Other Jews came flocking into Recife from different parts of Brazil which were still under Portuguese rule. They sent for a rabbi from Holland to teach them and to lead them in their prayers. They opened a house of worship. Many new settlers came from Hungary, Turkey and from the Germanic lands. Soon there were hundreds of Jews in Recife. They opened a second synagogue, bought more sugar mills, shipped their cargoes to Europe, imported

RECIFE, CENTER OF JEWISH LIFE IN BRAZIL
AFTER A CONTEMPORARY PAINTING

cloth, leather, furniture, silks, brocades. Recife became the most prosperous city in Brazil.

But in 1645 the Portuguese returned to take back Recife. Dutchmen and Jews fought side by side in the besieged city. When men fell at their posts, the women stepped in to take their places. The war dragged on for nine years, till food gave out and people began to die of starvation. At last the defenses of the city were broken and the Portuguese recaptured Recife.

The conquerors gave the Jews the choice of exile or

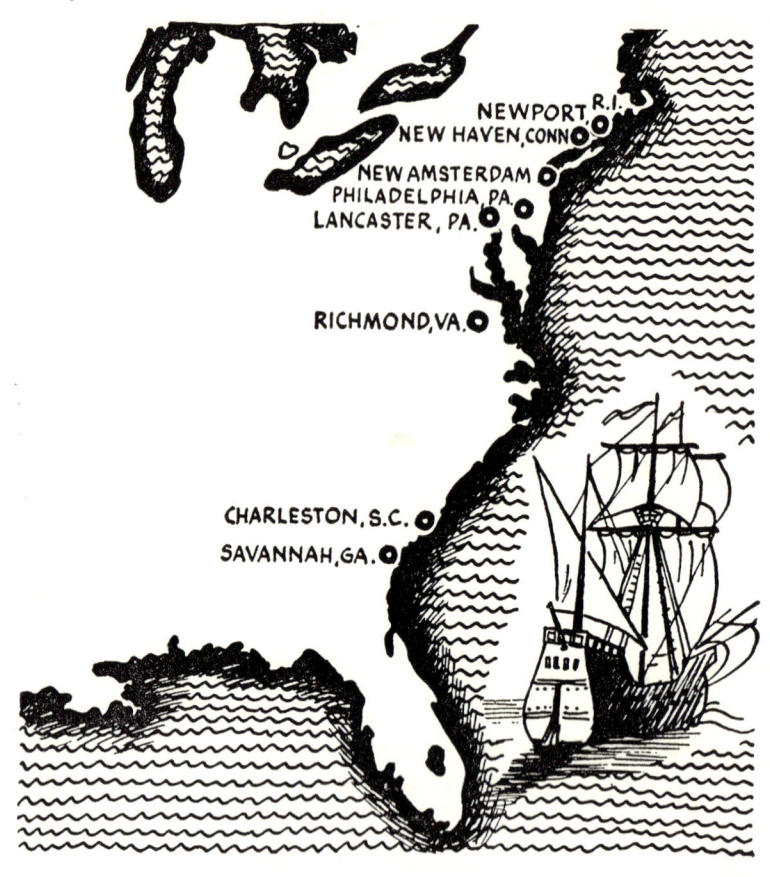

THE FIRST JEWISH SETTLEMENTS IN THE UNITED STATES

baptism, and the Jews chose exile. Hundreds returned to Holland. Some fled to Surinam, some to British Guiana, some to the West Indies.

To North America

Twenty-three sailed north. We do not know whether they intended to go north, or whether their ship was blown from its course. The group of twenty-three had many adventures. They were captured by pirates, and when it seemed there was no hope of reaching friendly shores, and that they would be sold as slaves, a French man-of-war, the St. Charles, hove into view. The St. Charles was a stout vessel, with cannon bristling from its gun ports. After a short battle the pirates were defeated, and the Jews were taken aboard the St. Charles.

They sailed north, along the shoreline of the North American continent. In the port of New Amsterdam, the first Dutch outpost on North American soil, the St. Charles came to berth. And here, in New Amsterdam, the Jewish refugees from Brazil made their homes.

Building a Country

As the North American continent slowly opened to settlers, thousands came sailing across the ocean from all parts of the Old World. They came because they were poor, because they were persecuted, because they wanted religious liberty, and sometimes, for pure love of adventure. But whatever the reasons that brought them, they built a new kind of life in America.

The Jews too kept coming, singly, in small groups, in waves. They helped roll back the wilderness. They helped build the colonies. They opened trails through forestland. They followed the wagon routes to the west. They helped build cities and develop commerce and cultivate fields.

The Jews helped build America. Together with all the American pioneers, they planted democracy.

For the Pupil

THINGS TO READ:

1. Leonard, Oscar, *Americans All*, Behrman House, New York, 1944, "Jews Helped Too," page 5, and "He Fought for His Rights," page 25.
2. Lurie, Rose, *The Great March*, Book Two, "Across the Sea," page 4, and "Land at Last," page 13.
3. Pessin, Deborah, *Giants on the Earth*, "Sail on, O My People," page 1.
4. Pessin, Deborah, *Michael Turns the Globe*, Union of American Hebrew Congregations, 1946, "In a Mexican Village," page 11.

THINGS TO TALK ABOUT:

1. How did the Jews contribute to the Renaissance?
2. Why were Jews so often among the first settlers in many lands of Europe as well as in the countries of the western hemisphere?

THINGS TO DO:

1. Write the story of a Jewish family who came from Holland to Brazil, then went on to New Amsterdam. If you like, illustrate your story.
2. Pretend you are one of the Jewish settlers in Recife. Write to a friend in Holland, telling him about life in the New World.

Teacher's Bibliography

Grayzel, Solomon, *A History of the Jews*, pp. 499-504.
Learsi, Rufus, *Israel*, pp. 394-395.
Marcus, Jacob Rader, *Early American Jewry*, Jewish Publication Society, 1951.

UNIT TWO

Light and Shadow in Poland

*T*HE JEWS of Eastern Europe developed a distinct way of life. It was a way of thinking, a way of feeling, a way of conducting themselves day by day. It made righteousness the highest goal, and scholarliness the highest office man could attain.

This way of life, which flourished for hundreds of years in Eastern Europe, brought the teachings of Judaism to their highest peak.

CHAPTER ONE

ᴡᴡ A Day in Lublin

In Feudal Poland

We now leave the New World, in which the Jews are settling with other pioneers, and return to a land in the Old World, where the Jews have been living for a number of centuries.

It is early in the seventeenth century when we visit Poland, a land of peasants and noblemen. Poland is still a feudal country, though some industry has been developed, and there are skilled craftsmen in the cities and villages. The bulk of Poland's population, however, is made up of poor peasants who cluster together in small villages. Overlooking the villages are the stately manors of the noblemen, with large cultivated parks and gardens, acres of forestland which provide game for the tables of the manors, shaded walks and rich orchards. The noblemen of Poland are only a handful in the large population. But they are the owners of the land, while the peasants are little more than serfs. They plow and plant the fields of the landowners, they gather their harvests, they pay them rent and taxes, they perform many services which the landowners expect as their due.

The Jews are widely scattered in this vast peasant population, sometimes living in the small villages, sometimes in the large cities. But wherever they live, they are organized into communities which they call *Kahals*. The leaders of each *Kahal* collect taxes from its members, so that they can provide for their rabbis, their teachers, run their schools, their hospitals, and take care of their poor. In each *Kahal* the Jews live according to their own laws, for the kings of Poland have granted them self-government. Aside from collecting taxes for the needs of their own communities, the *Kahals* also collect the government taxes, which are then passed on to government officials. So well do the Jews manage their own affairs, that their disputes are always settled by their own judges, their *Dayanim,* rather than in the Polish courts. Even Christians, in dispute with Jews, sometimes prefer taking their grievances to a Jewish court, which follows not the law of the land, but the law of the Talmud. The judge in the Jewish court is usually the rabbi of the town, and the Gentile who comes to him knows that he will receive justice, for the rabbi is above bribes, or corruption.

Let us visit a city in Poland on a spring day of the early seventeenth century, and see something of the life of the Jews in that country.

On the Roads to Lublin

The sun has barely risen as we approach the city of Lublin, and the air is sweet with the smell of melting snow and fresh earth. Lublin is holding her annual fair, and people are coming from far and near, from every city in Poland, and even from distant lands.

Along the roads leading to the gateway of Lublin,

wagons come rolling along. Many of these wagons carry Jews, for they too are eager to attend the famous fair. There are Jews in sheepskin coats and fur turbans and Jews in long black coats that are called *Kaftans*. There are Jews with pale blue eyes and wide cheekbones, like those of their Slavic neighbors, and Jews with black eyes and narrow faces. There are innkeepers, rabbis, traders, grain merchants, young students, and artisans of every kind. Some of them have been traveling for many days, stopping at inns to sleep and in fields to pray. Now they urge their horses on, flicking their sides with leather whips. There are many things they must do in Lublin before they return home.

How the Jews Came to Poland

The Jewish streets in Lublin are like human beehives. Greetings fly back and forth. *Shalom Aleikhem.* Peace

BRIDAL PAIR UNDER WEDDING CANOPY
FROM AN EMBROIDERED TORAH BAND

unto you. It is the old Hebrew greeting, centuries old, and it is used everywhere in the world. *Shalom Aleikhem.* Peace.

But Hebrew is not the everyday language of the Jews. The language they speak sounds like German, though it is different. The Germanic lands are just across the border, and during the crusades, when the Jews were attacked by crusaders on their march to Palestine, large groups of Jews fled to Poland. At the time of the Black Death, when Jews were accused of poisoning wells and were attacked by frenzied mobs, they came again to Poland.

Not all the Jews, however, came from the Germanic lands. Some drifted in many centuries before, at the very

WOODEN SYNAGOGUE IN POLAND (17th CENTURY)

A Day in Lublin

beginning of the Common Era. But most of the Jews came in later days, to escape the persecution they suffered in the Germanic lands.

The Polish kings welcomed the refugees and invited them to settle in Poland, granting them many rights and privileges. For Poland, in those early days, needed the skills which the Jews were able to provide. It was a land of peasants and nobility, with the noblemen owning the land and the peasants working for them. Between the nobility and the peasants there were scarcely any skilled workers, or merchants, or learned men. When the Jews came, they brought with them whatever they had learned in the west. They managed the estates of the noblemen. They opened stores, and villages sprang up around the stores. They brought in goods from other lands. They tilled the soil, manufactured clothes, shoes, leather goods, cloth, utensils.

The Language of the People

The Jews brought with them to Poland the German language, the language of the Germanic lands. Gradually, Hebrew words crept in. The pronunciation of some of the old German words was altered. The language developed into the language we call Yiddish, which became the folk language of the Jews of Poland. They talked in Yiddish, sang in Yiddish, wrote stories in Yiddish, printed books in Yiddish. And today, at the fair in Lublin early in the seventeenth century, we hear Yiddish on every side.

Finding a Rabbi

We make our way along the narrow, crowded streets. Everyone seems in high spirits. Everyone asks questions.

"Where do you hail from?"

"From the Ukraine, near the steppes. Ours is a new community."

"So."

"Only a handful of Jews."

"And do you have a synagogue?"

"We have a synagogue. Our nobleman gave us permission to build one. With our own hands we built it, so that our children may be Jews and study Torah."

"And a rabbi?"

"That is why I came to Lublin, to bring back a rabbi."

Lublin is famous for its Talmudical academy, or *Yeshivah*, and the fair always brings people in search of rabbis for their synagogues.

Goods for Sale

We elbow our way through the crowds. We see wagons filled with sacks of grain and wool, jugs of wine, kitchen utensils, sheepskin coats. Merchants display their goods attractively in stalls. There are rolls of silk and woolen cloth, leather boots hung up in rows, finely engraved Sabbath menorahs and *Kiddush* cups, copies of the Talmud which have been printed in Lublin. We see not only Jewish merchants, but merchants from Germany and from far-off Persia. The Persian merchants have brought tapestries and rugs and ornaments made of ivory.

Trade is brisk. Noblemen with feathers in their hats buy large stocks of supplies for their larders and tapestries for their ballrooms. Silks, furniture, books, grain, quickly change hands. Women move through the throngs, bright kerchiefs on their heads and baskets on their arms.

Finding a Bridegroom

But not every Jew who has come to Lublin has come to buy or sell, or to bring back a rabbi for his community. There are students who have come to enroll in the famous *Yeshivah*, and merchants who have come to find bridegrooms for their daughters.

There, beside a wagon filled with boots, we see a father who has brought his sixteen year old son to be enrolled in the academy. The father is praising his son to a rich merchant, who keeps eyeing the embarrassed youth.

"Hmm," says the merchant, whose cheeks are as round and red as apples. "You have raised a fine son."

"He will be a great rabbi in Israel," the father proudly predicts. "Already the lad knows fifty pages of the Talmud by heart."

"God has not blessed me with sons," the merchant sighs heavily. "But I have a daughter whose beauty is like the sun. Yet she is modest, gentle—"

"And how old is your daughter?" asks the father, as his son pretends not to hear.

"Fourteen, and already the matchmaker gives us no rest. But I vowed that I would marry her only to a brilliant *Yeshivah* student."

"And her dowry?" the boy's father asks, as his son's ears burn with embarrassment.

"I am a rich man," the merchant says, "and I have only my daughter to care for."

And the rich merchant and the proud father walk off together to find a quiet spot where they can discuss the engagement of their children. The boy, left to himself, strolls about among the stalls, a shy smile on his lips.

Rich fathers do not always find student husbands for their daughters at the fair. Usually they go straight to the *Yeshivah* and seek out the most brilliant students there. The Jews of Poland prize learning above everything. Their nobility does not consist of kings and princes and noblemen. The *Yeshivah* students, spending their days and nights over the pages of the Talmud, are the Jewish nobility.

The Council of the Four Lands

In a house on one of the Jewish streets, an important meeting is taking place. It is a meeting of the *Va'ad Arba Aratzot*, the Council of the Four Lands. The four "lands" which the *Va'ad* represents are the main provinces of Poland—Great Poland, Little Poland, Galicia, Volyhnia.

Each year, when Lublin holds its spring fair, every important *Kahal* sends a representative to the *Va'ad*. For there might be an important matter that concerns the Jews of all of Poland. Or there might be a dispute between two *Kahals*. Or a man might have a grievance against his *Kahal*. So the Jews of Poland created their *Va'ad* to unite them into one body.

Let us pretend we are attending a meeting of the *Va'ad*. We enter the house where the *Va'ad* is assembled, and we find that there are thirty delegates, all sitting together in a room. Six of them are famous rabbis, and the rest are important laymen.

A Shtadlan

A man from a distant town is talking to members of the *Va'ad*. Reb Joseph made the long trip to Lublin to tell them something which he knows will delight them. They listen intently, their eyes fixed on Reb Joseph.

It seems that a nobleman, a member of Parliament, tried to have a law passed which was unfavorable to the Jews. If the law had been passed, it would have meant

A Day in Lublin

that Jews must keep their stores and shops closed on Sunday. Since the Jews kept their stores closed on their own Sabbath, this would have meant that they must cease doing business for two days instead of one. Obviously, says Reb Joseph, this nobleman meant to impoverish the Jews.

But luckily, he goes on, Reb Samuel got wind of what he was planning, and away he went to Cracow, where Parliament met. Reb Samuel appointed himself his people's *Shtadlan,* or representative. "And who," demands Reb Joseph, "could have been a better *Shtadlan?*" For Reb Samuel speaks Polish well. He is a good diplomat, knowing how to turn prejudice into friendship. And besides, he knows many noblemen personally.

"To make a long story short," says Reb Joseph, "Reb Samuel worked day and night, never resting, talking to his noblemen friends, arguing, pleading, persuading. And in the end," he says with a beaming face, "the law was not passed."

The members of the *Va'ad* sit back in their chairs.

"Well done," one of them says. "Thank God there was a Reb Samuel to save us in the nick of time."

"For every Haman who rises against us," another says, "we manage to bring forth a Mordecai."

"We must send Reb Samuel a letter thanking him for what he has done for the Jews of Poland," says one of the rabbis. "Reb Joseph, will you be our messenger?"

"Willingly," says Joseph, rising from his chair. "I will spend a few hours at the fair, then I will return for the letter."

And Joseph leaves to visit the fair, happy at the impression his story has made on the *Va'ad*.

Who Is a Jew?

Now a man enters the room with a letter in his hand. The man is from the city of Brest, and the letter he carries is from the rabbi of his *Kahal*. He murmurs a greeting as he hands over the letter and remains standing as one of the members of the *Va'ad* reads the letter aloud.

"We have among us," the letter says, "a family which has migrated from a distant land. This family claims to be Jewish. Their names, we admit, are Jewish names, Jacob, Judith, and Esther. But we suspect they are not Jewish, for despite their names—"

"What is this?" says the reader of the letter, throwing it down on the table. "What kind of a letter have you brought us?"

"The letter is from our rabbi," the man answers. "We do not know what to do."

"What is there to do?"

"We suspect that the family pretends to be Jewish."

"What makes you think they are pretending?"

"We have reason to suspect it. We—"

"But what right have you to suspect any such thing? Why should they pretend?"

"Heaven knows why they should pretend, but we are not sure they are Jews. We questioned them, and they did not even know the Hebrew names of their parents."

"But you had no right to question them," another mem-

MEETING PLACE OF THE COUNCIL OF THE FOUR LANDS IN LUBLIN

ber of the *Va'ad* breaks in. "If they had wanted to lie, could they not have invented names for their parents?"

The man hesitates, seems about to speak, remains silent.

"If they say they are Jews, they are Jews," a *Va'ad* member declares flatly. "You have no right to question them about their parents or their past. And they are to enjoy the right of every other member of the community. If you like, we will give you a letter to your rabbi, with our decision."

But the man from Brest does not wait for a letter. He leaves the room more quickly than he entered it, his face flushed. His place is soon taken by another man who approaches the *Va'ad* slowly, for he is not accustomed to speaking to so important a gathering.

An Unfair Tax

The newcomer has come to complain about the taxes his *Kahal* imposes upon the poor people.

"It is not fair," he protests. "The tax is too high. I am

only a miller. I make barely enough to support my family, and to pay a reasonable tax."

"Why do you consider the tax unreasonable?" he is asked. "Every *Kahal* must tax its members, or nothing could be done."

"I understand," says the miller. "But it is not fair to tax salt. I pay as much as the rich, because I must have my salt as well as they. Salt is a necessity."

"He is right," says a *Va'ad* member. "Salt is a necessity and should not be taxed."

"Why not tax meat instead of salt?" another member

PURIM PLATE
KIDDUSH CUP
CANDLESTICK
(GERMANY, 18th CENT.)

asks. "The rich eat more meat than the poor. They would therefore pay a higher tax than the poor."

The miller nods his head in agreement, and the *Va'ad* promises him that they will write a letter to the *Kahal*, suggesting a tax on meat instead of on salt. The miller goes out satisfied. He knows that a suggestion from the *Va'ad* is as good as law.

The Stubborn Merchant

It is growing late, and the *Va'ad* has time for one more case before it retires for the day. This time it is the *Kahal* of Jaroslaw which is complaining against one of its members. The *Dayanim*, or judges of the *Kahal* of Jaroslaw are not sure whether they are right in their judgment, so one of them has come to Lublin, to present the case to the *Va'ad*.

"There is a rich merchant who lives among us," says

the *Dayan* of Jaroslaw, "who is a thorn in our side."

A member of the *Va'ad* smiles and says, "We cannot always get rid of our thorns."

The *Dayan* smiles too, then his face hardens and he says, "This merchant deals with Spain."

"With Spain?"

"He sells goods to Spain, and thereby grows rich."

There is no sign of a smile now anywhere. A rabbi leans forward and asks, "You mean that he finds it in his heart to send goods to a country that tortured and exiled our people?"

"We argued with him. We spent a day arguing. We almost came to blows. But what could we do? He claims that it is legal. And naturally, there is no Jewish law to forbid it."

"Does not his heart forbid it?"

The judge of Jaroslaw shrugs his shoulders. "The man has a heart. That I admit. He contributes liberally whenever he is called upon, even more than we ask. There is no poor bride among us to whose dowry he does not contribute. Four *Yeshivah* students eat at his table. But he insists that there is no law that forbids trade with Spain."

"If he has a heart," says a rabbi of the *Va'ad,* "you must speak to it. Speak to him gently, as a father speaks to his son. Tell him of Spain's crimes against his people. He will listen when he knows. Our books have no law against trading with Spain. You must plant the law in his heart."

The *Dayan* is impressed with the gentle earnestness of the rabbi. If he could only speak to the merchant in such a way, without losing his head! He determines that he

A Day in Lublin

will succeed, and he leaves the *Va'ad* and goes out into the street, where twilight has already fallen.

The day is almost over. The fair is closed. Tomorrow it will reopen. Fathers will enroll their sons in the *Yeshivah*. Members of the *Kahals* will choose rabbis to bring home with them. Merchants will seek wise students for their daughters. And the *Va'ad* will meet again to pass ordinances, to settle cases, and to look after the interests of their people.

For the Pupil

THINGS TO TALK ABOUT:

1. Compare Jewish life in early America with Jewish life in feudal Poland.
2. Why did the early kings of Poland welcome the Jews?
3. Why did the kings of Poland permit the Jews their own internal government?
4. Why did the Jews prefer to rule themselves?

THINGS TO DO:

1. Make up a few cases to be brought before the *Va'ad*.
2. Act out your cases.
3. Do a painting of the fair in Lublin.

Teacher's Bibliography

Grayzel, Solomon, *A History of the Jews*, pp. 443-452.
Learsi, Rufus, *Israel*, pp. 345-354.
Margolis and Marx, *History of the Jewish People*, pp. 525-546.

CHAPTER TWO

〰️ A Nation of Students

The Gateway into Poland

We now leave the city of Lublin and make our way to Cracow, Poland's capital city. Travel is slow, and we stop at many towns, so that we do not reach the capital till Shavuot, the Feast of Weeks, which commemorates the giving of the Torah.

Cracow is not far from the border of the Germanic lands. That is why many Jews, fleeing from the Germanic lands, have settled in Cracow. They run stores and inns and mills. They trade in furs, grain, wine, cattle, lumber. They manufacture goods and import and export. Some of them are agents for the noblemen, who seem to do nothing but hunt, sleep, eat and drink. The noblemen have large estates which need care, and in order to live their lives of luxury, they must collect rent and taxes from the peasants. This work, the management of their estates and the collection of rent and taxes, the noblemen have handed over to the Jews, for they find the Jews honest and efficient.

It is still early morning when we reach Cracow, and as we stroll through the streets we try to pick out the Jews of the city. This is easy to do, for despite the fact that the Jews are not required to wear badges on their clothes to set them apart from their neighbors, as is true in the Germanic lands, the Jews in Poland wear beards and earlocks. It is especially easy to pick out the *Baḥurim,* the *Yeshivah* students who are on their way to the *Yeshivah.* There is the look of the student about them, and because they spend many hours indoors over the Talmud, their faces do not have the ruddiness of outdoor life.

Going to School

What interests us particularly this morning are the very young boys we see here and there—they cannot be more than five or six—who walk so solemnly down the street, each boy at the side of a man. We know that the boys are Jewish, for the men who walk beside them seem to be rabbis, or at least very learned men. The men look like *Yeshivah* students grown older, graver and wiser.

Let us pretend that we fall into step beside one of the boys and his escort. We learn that this is the child's first day at school, or *Ḥeder*. That is why his clothes are new and he looks so scrubbed. The man's name is Reb Jonah, and as we supposed, he is a scholar and much respected in the community. A child's first day at school is so important that Reb Jonah came to the boy's house to take him there. Shavuot, the festival which commemorates the giving of the Torah, is the time when children go to *Ḥeder* for the first time. All through Cracow, all through Lublin, all through Poland, boys who have reached the age of five are off to school, each child scrubbed and glowing with happiness.

The name of the boy we are walking with is Daniel, and we know, merely from looking at his face, that he can hardly contain his feeling of importance. To *Ḥeder* at last, like his big brother, who goes to the *Yeshivah* of Cracow! Daniel's mother is at home, preparing the feast that will be held when he returns home. And Daniel, like a grown man, is off to study Torah.

Torah and Honey

But here we are at *Ḥeder,* which is a room in the home of the teacher. Daniel's teacher, a middle-aged man, is at the door to greet his new student. Daniel's parents can afford to pay tuition and they have chosen Reb Moses to be their child's teacher. Children whose parents cannot afford to pay tuition attend the Talmud Torah, which is supported by the community.

We enter Reb Moses' house and he leads us into a room which has benches on both sides of a long table. Reb Moses has about twenty-five students and two assistants. But neither assistants nor children are in school today. They are at home, celebrating the festival of Shavuot.

The teacher strokes Daniel's head, for now that he is in *Ḥeder,* the child seems a bit frightened. Reb Moses tells Daniel that there is nothing to fear. Then he hands the child a slate, and on it we see the letters of the Hebrew alphabet. There are also some Hebrew verses about the Torah. One of the verses reads: "The Law commanded us by Moses is the inheritance of the Congregation of Israel." After Daniel has repeated the letters after the teacher, the slate is covered with honey. As Daniel licks the honey from the letters he tastes the sweetness of the Torah.

Daniel is then given a cake which, like the slate, has verses from the Bible traced upon it. One of the verses reads: "How sweet are Thy words unto my taste! Yea, sweeter than honey to my mouth!"

The teacher takes Daniel onto his lap and reads the verses, and the child carefully repeats them after him, word by word. Daniel is now told that he may eat the cake, as well as other sweets which have been provided for him. This Daniel promptly does, smiling happily as he eats.

When the little meal is over, Daniel's escort takes his hand and leaves the *Heder* with him, and we go along to see what they will do now.

Where the Torah Rests

To our astonishment, we are led to the outskirts of the city, to a wide green meadow. We wander through the meadow till we come to a stream, and as we walk along its bank, Reb Jonah says to the little boy, "Notice how the water runs between its banks, always downward."

"Yes," says Daniel, looking at the stream, "it runs down, down, down, till it gathers and becomes a pool."

"It comes to rest," says Reb Jonah, "in a low place, for water never flows upward, only downward."

"BAR MITZVAH"
after a painting by Moritz Oppenheim

The lad looks up at the scholar questioningly, wondering what all this has to do with Torah, or with school.

"So it is with the Torah," says Reb Jonah. "We do not find it among the haughty and the proud, but among the modest and humble. And so, my child, you must be always modest and humble in your ways."

We finish our stroll in the cool, green meadow and return to the city. Soon Daniel is at home, where the guests who have been invited to the feast greet him as he enters. "May God enlighten thine eyes with the Torah," they say.

As we turn to go, we catch a glimpse, through the window, of bright-cheeked women with lace caps on their heads, of gleaming silverware and vases of flowers. Daniel's happy voice, as he tells about his first day at *Ḥeder*, follows us as we stroll down the street in the fresh sunlight.

The Yeshivah

Daniel will study Hebrew reading, the prayers and the Bible at *Ḥeder*. He will study many hours each day, from morning till night. When he is ten, he will begin the study of the Talmud, and by the time he is thirteen he will be through with *Ḥeder*. Then, if he is a good student, he will go on to the *Yeshivah*, like his brother Aaron.

Aaron, who is fifteen, takes his studies seriously. It is not because he wants to be a rabbi that he attends the academy. It is because he has been brought up to love his studies.

Aaron is fortunate. Poland is dotted with *Yeshivot*, so that any boy who wishes can study at one of them. But the *Yeshivah* of Cracow, like the one of Lublin, is one of the best in the land. Often boys come from far away, even from distant lands, to study at a famous *Yeshivah*. Often they come penniless, with only the clothes they are wearing. But they know they will be taken care of.

The *Yeshivah* is supported by the community, and there is a special room in it where boys away from home can sleep. Some of the students also have their meals at the *Yeshivah*. Besides, the people consider it a *Mitzvah*, a good deed, to have a *Yeshivah Baḥur* at their table. Reb Abraham, for example, will invite the *Baḥur*, Nathan, to eat at his house every Saturday. Simon the weaver tells Nathan that he expects him at his home every Sunday. On Monday, Nathan eats his dinner at the home of Reb Jonah. For each day of the week the *Baḥur* has a different home to provide his food. This is called *Essen Teg*, which means, eating days, and it is a widespread custom in Poland. Sometimes a *Baḥur* marries the daughter of one of his hosts. Then, of course, the bride brings him a dowry, and he lives at the home of her parents till his studies are over, or until he is ready to set up his own home.

The Baḥurim

We visit the *Yeshivah* of Cracow, one day, to see what it is like. The *Yeshivah*, we find, is also used as a synagogue, and it has a number of rooms opening onto a large vestibule. As we enter the building we hear the sound of young, chanting voices, and we need no guide to tell us whose voices these are. We walk in the direction of the voices and soon we find ourselves among a group of *Baḥurim*.

The room has no adornments. Whitewashed walls, long tables, benches, a few stands. Some of the students seem very young, fourteen or fifteen. Some are in their twenties. Here a group is seated at a table, each one with a Talmud open before him. The rabbi has assigned them a passage to study, and they must know it thoroughly by the time he comes to examine them. So they are busily at work, chanting the words of the Talmud as they sway back and forth, back and forth, as though the swaying and the chanting go together. Strangely enough, the rabbi can tell from the way a student chants the passage whether he really understands it.

Here, a *Baḥur* stands by himself over his copy of the Talmud. He is chanting the words of a difficult passage which he is determined to master. So deeply immersed is he in his studies, that the voices of the others do not disturb him, though the passage he is studying is not the same as theirs.

Three students are standing in a corner of the room. They seem to be about eighteen, and they are discussing a law they have been studying in the Talmud. The law reminds them of a story, found in the Midrash, which one of the *Bahurim* tells.

A Nation of Students

When God wanted to give the Jews the Torah, the story goes, He looked around for a mountain from which He could hand it down to Israel. The lofty mountains quarreled, for each wanted to be chosen by God. But there was one mountain, not as grand and lofty as the others, which was silent, for it did not consider itself worthy of being chosen by God for handing down the Torah. This was Mount Sinai, and it was this mountain that God chose, because of its modesty. The story reminds us, in turn, of what Reb Jonah told Daniel in the meadow, that the Torah rests with the modest and humble.

On through the day the boys discuss and study, today and every day. On and on and on, till the small hours of the night, when they study by candlelight. These slender, pale-faced boys are the pride of their people. Yet they are not proud. For they have been taught that they must not use the Torah as a crown.

For the Pupil

THINGS TO TALK ABOUT:

1. Why was study so important to the Jews of Poland?
2. Why were the Bible and the Talmud treasured by the Jews scattered over the world?
3. What does this sentence mean: "They have been taught that they must not use the Torah as a crown"?

THINGS TO DO:

1. Your grandfather or grandmother may have come from a town in Poland or Russia. Ask them to tell you about the Jewish schools there. Perhaps your grandfather would like to come and tell all your classmates about his school days, about *Essen Teg*, about life in general.
2. Ask your rabbi if he would like to visit your class and tell you some stories from the Talmud and the Midrash.

Teacher's Bibliography

Ginzburg, Louis, *Students, Scholars and Saints*, Jewish Publication Society, 1928, "The Jewish Primary School," pp. 1-34.
Grayzel, Solomon, *A History of the Jews*, pp. 452-459; 505-508.

CHAPTER THREE

The False Messiah

In the Ukraine

In the south of Poland, among the Ukrainian people, there lived many Cossack peasants. The Ukraine had been conquered by Poland, and the Cossacks of the Ukraine felt no love for their conquerors. The Cossacks considered themselves related to the Russians, not to the Poles. Yet like the Polish peasants, they paid rent and taxes to the Polish noblemen. Even the religion of the Cossacks was different from the religion of the Poles, for while the Cossacks, like the Russians, were Greek Orthodox Christians, the Poles were Roman Catholics. Each time the Cossacks had to use their churches, they were forced to pay their Polish landlords a tax.

The Jews of Poland were caught between the noblemen and the peasants, for some Jews were the agents who collected the taxes and the rent. The Cossacks hated the Jewish agents even more than they hated the Poles. They never saw the noblemen, who were usually in Cracow, enjoying the life of the capital, or were busy hunting and banqueting. But the Jews were always among them, doing the work of the noblemen. The Jewish agents had even been given the keys to the Greek Orthodox churches, so that when the Cossacks wanted to use their own churches, they had to ask the Jewish agents for the keys, and hand over a tax. The Cossacks did not consider that the Jews were acting for the noblemen, and not for themselves. They knew only that they had to pay taxes to the Jews, even for the right to use their churches.

The Revolt of the Cossacks

In the year 1648, rebellion broke over the Ukraine. In that year a Cossack leader called Chmelnitzki raised the standard of revolt. He had carefully prepared for the revolt, and behind him stood thousands of swift-riding Cossacks from beyond the Dnieper. He had also made an alliance with the Tatars, reckless warriors of the Crimea. Declaring that he would free the Ukrainians from their oppressors, he met the Polish army and defeated it.

With Chmelnitzki's first success, Cossack peasants rose on every side to join his forces. They formed into bands and swept westward and northward over Poland, killing

Jews and Poles wherever they met them. But though many Poles lost their lives in the Chmelnitzki revolt, the full fury and hatred of the Cossacks were spent upon the Jews.

For years the massacres continued. Jews died in the thousands. To escape the cruelty of the Cossacks, Jews often fled to the Tatars, who sold them as slaves to Turkey. But here they were ransomed by their people, while in Poland the massacres continued.

In 1651, a new, strong Polish army prepared to meet Chmelnitzki. The Cossack leader suffered defeat, and it seemed that the end of the uprisings had come. But Chmelnitzki made an alliance with the Czar of Russia, and the armies of the Czar, together with the Cossacks, marched into Poland. Again the massacres began, and again thousands of Jews were wiped out.

When the storm was over at last, in the year 1660, and Poland had freed herself of invaders, it was found that half a million Jews had died. Families had been scattered, communities had vanished, synagogues and schools had been razed to the ground. The *Va'ad Arba Aratzot* tried to mend what had been broken. It tried to gather the broken threads, to unite the scattered families and rebuild the *Kahals*. But the terror and the fury of the Cossacks had been too great. The blooming years of the Jews in Poland were over.

Sabbatai Zevi

As always, when the suffering was great, the Jews asked, when will the Messiah come?

And even as they asked the question, rumors began to spread. North, east, south and west, the rumors were carried. The Messiah has come!

The man who had proclaimed himself the Messiah was Sabbatai Zevi. He was born in the year 1626, in the city of Smyrna, in Turkey. Like every Jewish boy, he was sent to school. But as he grew older he became more and more interested in the *Kabbalah*. Then young Sabbatai began to live in a world of fancy, and because he was handsome and his manner was pleasing, he drew many youths around him. They looked upon him as their leader, for Sabbatai was a fiery and convincing speaker.

When Sabbatai Zevi was twenty-two years old, he stood up before the Torah in the synagogue and pronounced the name of God. Now this was never done by the Jews, for they considered God's name too sacred to be spoken by man, except after the coming of the Messiah. Did Sabbatai, then, dare consider himself the Messiah? The rabbis of Smyrna, horrified at Sabbatai's daring, excommunicated him.

Sabbatai went to Salonika, where he gathered a group of men, students of both the Talmud and the *Kabbalah*. Under their astonished eyes, Sabbatai "married" himself to the Torah by standing under a wedding canopy with the Torah in his arms. But this horrified the Jews of Salonika as the pronouncement of God's name had horrified the Jews of Smyrna. Sabbatai was banished from Salonika, and he went from place to place, attracting followers as he went.

Wherever he went, tall, handsome, serene, they surrounded him, eager for his words and the beauty of his voice when he sang. A rich man of Cairo sent Sabbatai to Jerusalem with money for the poor, and there too people flocked about him, attracted by his lordly bearing and his words of mystery. He returned to Cairo, and his followers declared openly that Sabbatai Zevi was the Messiah.

Sabbatai's Bride

There lived in Poland a beautiful young woman whose name was Sarah. Both her parents had died in the Cossack wars. One day, Sarah was found wandering in a cemetery where, she said, the spirit of her father had led her. She was destined, she said, to be the bride of the Messiah.

When Sabbatai Zevi, who was in Cairo, heard of the beautiful maiden, he sent for her and made her his bride. Then more and more people flocked to Sabbatai Zevi. For did it not prove that he was the Messiah when he married a maiden who had predicted that she would be the wife of the Messiah?

SABBATAI ZEVI

SABBATAI ZEVI PICTURED WITH HIS DISCIPLES
FROM AN AMSTERDAM PRAYERBOOK

Preparing for the Messiah

What had been whispered was now spoken aloud, more and more boldly. The Messiah is truly here, thousands of people said. Through Europe, Asia, Africa, the news ran, and men and women cried for joy. Messiah has come! Printing presses were kept busy turning out prayer books, for never before had there been so much praying. People danced in the streets. They sold their goods, so that they would be ready to follow the Messiah when he came for them. Men fasted and prayed so that they would be cleansed of all sin.

And miracle stories began to spread.

Newborn babes speak Sabbatai's name.

The dead rise from their graves and proclaim him.

He will gather the Ten Lost Tribes and bring them to Zion.

He sailed with a crew and no captain. He sailed with

The False Messiah

an escort of four hundred prophets, and a pillar of fire descended from heaven and enveloped the ship.

In triumph, Sabbatai Zevi returned to Smyrna, his native city. Crowds lined the streets to see him pass.

"Long live our King, our Anointed One!" they cried.

Through the crowds Sabbatai walked, tall and stately and handsome. Beside him walked his bride, dressed all in white. And as he walked he sang, "The right hand of the Lord is exalted; the right hand of the Lord doeth valiantly." At the sound of his clear, beautiful voice, the people went wild with joy.

The End

But the sultan did not like the excitement Sabbatai Zevi was causing. For Turks too had closed their stores and were waiting for the Messiah. Christians and Mohammedans as well as Jews were caught up in the excitement. Business in Turkey was almost at a standstill, and there was unrest among the people.

The sultan sent for Sabbatai Zevi. Sabbatai Zevi sailed for Constantinople, and when he arrived he was led in chains to prison. But even in prison Sabbatai Zevi bore himself like a king. Gifts poured in from all parts of the world. Pilgrims came from Poland, Germany, Italy, Holland to see him and to kiss the hem of his robe. The excitement was even greater than it had been before.

The sultan sent for Sabbatai Zevi to appear before him. It is told that the sultan ordered Sabbatai to prove he was the Messiah by jumping into a fire. If he refused to do this, he must accept Mohammedanism.

As his loyal followers watched him anxiously, Sabbatai stood motionless, for a moment, before the sultan. Then slowly, he raised his hands to his head and removed his Jewish headdress. And in the dead silence that filled the room, he put a Turkish turban on his head.

Sabbatai Zevi had chosen Mohammedanism. Still some of his followers could not believe that he had betrayed them. They claimed that they had heard a voice from heaven declare that the time was not ripe for the Messiah, and that Sabbatai's soul had ascended to heaven, so that it was but an ordinary mortal who had accepted Mohammedanism.

But most of his followers realized that Sabbatai Zevi had proved to be a false Messiah. In all the countries of the world, the Jews wept with shame and sorrow. For their hope of peace and justice had died.

Despair

After Sabbatai Zevi died, other men arose who claimed they were the Messiah. They appeared now in one country, now in another, and some of them said that they were Sabbatai Zevi come to life again. But they too proved to be false Messiahs.

In the parts of Poland where the massacres had been heaviest, the despair of the Jews was greatest. Their communities had been almost entirely destroyed. Their great academies were gone. Sabbatai Zevi had failed them. There was only poverty and gloom about them. They had been abandoned, they felt, both by man and by God. How could they be Jews, they asked, without their schools? How could they know God's will, if they could no longer read the books that taught them His will?

But in the darkness of their despair, a man came to comfort them. It is not the learned man alone who can know God, he said. For God, said the Baal Shem Tov, is interested in every human being, however humble. The poor cobbler, the weaver, the woodchopper, can be as pleasing in God's sight as the scholar who sits over the heavy tomes of the Talmud.

For the Pupil

THINGS TO READ:

1. Kalischer, Betty, *Watchmen of the Night,* "The Day of Judgment," page 117.
2. Levinger, Elma, *Great Jews Since Bible Times,* "The Turkish Messiah," page 4.
3. Lurie, Rose, *The Great March,* Book Two, "On the Wings of a Dragon," page 30.
4. Pessin, Deborah, *Giants on the Earth,* "The Hope That Failed," page 30.

THINGS TO TALK ABOUT:

1. How were the Jews caught between the noblemen and the peasants of Poland?
2. Discuss the Jewish conception of the Messiah. Can you mention other times, aside from the time of Sabbatai Zevi, when the Jews longed for the Messiah? What were the conditions which made dreaming of the Messiah natural?

THINGS TO DO:

1. Dramatize one of the stories listed under THINGS TO READ.
2. Write a story about a family in Poland that prepared to follow Sabbatai Zevi.

Teacher's Bibliography

Ash, Sholom, *Kiddush Ha-Shem,* Jewish Publication Society, 1936.

Grayzel, Solomon, *A History of the Jews,* pp. 509-520.

Learsi, Rufus, *Israel,* pp. 354-369.

Margolis and Marx, *History of the Jewish People,* pp. 551-567.

CHAPTER FOUR

ᴡᴡ The Rise of Ḥasidism

A Boy Called Israel

In a town in the south of Poland, in a region of the country where the Cossacks had brought great destruction, a child was born in about the year 1700. His parents called the child Israel, and when the boy was still very young, they died. Israel was taken care of by the community. The villagers fed the lad, clothed him and sent him to Ḥeder.

But Israel was not a student after their hearts. He preferred the woods to his hard bench at school, and often he would slip away and wander through the woods for hours at a time.

When Israel grew older, he became a teacher's assistant. His duties were to bring the very young children to Ḥeder, take them home again, and help them rehearse the alphabet and the simple prayers. Israel lived contentedly, for his needs were simple.

The Lime Digger

The youth became a man, and Israel married and went to live near the Carpathian Mountains. To earn a living, he dug lime from the mountains and carted it to the village to be sold. Though he lived humbly with his wife, he was happy, for he loved the wild, beautiful country of the Carpathian Mountains. He loved the simple majesty of the hills, the trees and the sky. He felt that God was in everything about him, in the tiny insects as in the lofty mountains, in the clod of earth as in the rushing waters.

At night, when his work was done, Israel would shut himself up in his rooms and study and pray. And he would sit for hours trying to understand the meaning of God and prayer, and the love that filled his heart for the people about him.

Several years went by, and Israel and his wife went to a town to live. His wife's brother, who was a rabbi, had been displeased when his sister had married Israel, whom he considered an ignorant man. But he pitied his

TRADITIONAL PICTURE OF THE BAAL SHEM TOV

sister for her poverty, and he gave her money to open an inn. While his wife took care of the inn, Israel secretly devoted himself to his studies.

The Teacher

Because Israel always radiated contentment and happiness, people came to him when they were in trouble, or when they wanted help or advice. They came to him for comfort, and for remedies when they were ill. As more and more people came to know Israel, a group of students gradually gathered about him. His students called their master Rabbi Israel, and they soon found that he had something to teach them that they had never heard taught before.

Israel taught his followers joy and happiness. It was not only the learned man, he taught them, who could be close to God. For God loved everyone, those who were learned as well as those who were not. Nor was it necessary to be a scholar to know God's will. For God was everywhere, in whatever man touched or felt or saw. Simple prayers were enough to reach God, if one's heart was in the prayers. Joy, said Israel, was the highest form of worship, joy in living as well as joy in prayer.

As often happens with great men, legends began to grow up about him. Israel was the Master of God's Name, people said, and by uttering God's Name, he could heal the sick and perform great miracles for his people. And they called him the Baal Shem Tov, Good Master of the Name, while his followers, who lived pious lives, were called *Ḥasidim*, which means pious men.

The Spread of Hasidism

It was at this time that Poland was gradually losing her strength. The peasants were impoverished by years of war. The noblemen, unable to rule wisely, were doing nothing to protect their land from her neighbors. One weak king followed another. Eventually, at the end of the eighteenth century, Russia, Austria and Germany stepped in and divided Poland amongst themselves.

With the gradual weakening of Poland and with the destruction brought by the Chmelnitzki revolt, came a steady weakening of Jewish life. The *Va'ad Arba Aratzot* by this time was gone. Rich *Kahals* had become poor communities. Many academies had disappeared. The people felt only cold poverty and despair. Now came Ḥasidism with its warm message of joy. Wherever it reached, it brought with it a feeling of hope. The people were comforted for the destruction of their bustling *Kahals* and famous academies. The poor man, scarcely able to earn a living, felt that he was no longer abandoned. For was he not as important to God as the wise rabbis and the scholars who could read the books of the Talmud? So warm and joyous were the teachings of the Baal Shem Tov, that not only the poor and the ignorant, but students and rabbis too were caught up in the movement of *Ḥasidism* that swept over Eastern Europe.

Tales of Wonder

Many beautiful stories did the *Ḥasidim* weave about their beloved teacher. Such fanciful tales had not been told for hundreds of years, since the days of the Talmud. Now again, in the dreary little villages of Poland, tales of wonder were spun endlessly about the kindly teacher who was bidding the shoemaker, the water-carrier, the waggoner, the woodchopper, dance and rejoice and be merry. The way to worship God, said the Baal Shem Tov, was with song and dance. So the *Ḥasidic* houses of worship resounded with the sound of their dancing feet and the happy songs they sang. And when the *Ḥasidim* prayed, they prayed with all their hearts, as the Baal Shem Tov had taught. And often, their eyes dilated with wonder, they told one another the stories they had heard about the Baal Shem Tov, each story teller adding his bit to what he had heard.

Many a time, they said, the Baal Shem Tov struggled with Satan, the Prince of Evil. And always it was the Baal Shem Tov who won the struggle. It happened once that great suffering came to the Jews. For Satan, employing all the spirits of evil, blocked the roads that led to God's throne, so that the prayers of the Jews could not reach Him. The prayers lay in heaps where they had been thrust by the evil spirits, whimpering and helpless. And on earth, the suffering grew greater.

At last the Baal Shem Tov himself went up and battled with the evil spirits and with Satan. And though he was one against many, he overcame them all and opened the gates that led to the throne of God. And the prayers rushed in through the open gates, and the suffering of the Jews ended on earth.

When the Baal Shem Tov prayed, said the *Ḥasidim*, his fervor was so great that anything that was near him trembled.

Once, said a disciple of the Baal Shem Tov, he was with the Baal Shem Tov as he stood praying at the east

A HASID WITH HIS WIFE
(EARLY 19TH CENTURY, FROM HOLLAENDERSKI: "LES ISRAÉLITES DE POLOGNE")

wall of a room. At the west wall stood a barrel of grain. And the disciple saw the grain in the barrel trembling.

Rabbi Israel and a group of his disciples were travelling along a road. It was a day in winter, the story went, and the wagon creaked along the icy road. When evening came, the Baal Shem Tov ordered that the horses be stopped so that they could descend and pray. So numb with cold were the disciples, that they could scarcely stand upright. Rabbi Israel went to a tree and touched it. The tree burst into flame. The *Hasidim* gathered around the tree and prayed, the flames warming their cold bodies. Then they got into the wagon and continued their journey.

For centuries the tales went on and on, growing in number, each generation of *Hasidim* adding to them and handing them down to the next generation. Not only about the Baal Shem Tov did they weave their tales, but about other great *Hasidic* leaders who followed him. And as time went by, the songs, the dances, and the stories became part of the culture not only of the *Hasidim*, but of all the Jews.

Changes in Ḥasidism

After Israel's death, changes crept into his teachings. The leaders of the *Ḥasidim* were called *Tzadikim*, or righteous men. Though many were pious, sincere leaders, like the Baal Shem Tov, there were some who ruled their followers almost like kings. The position of the *Tzadik* was hereditary, passing on from father to son, and it did not matter if the son was not as pious as his father. The ordinary *Ḥasidim*, the cobblers, the weavers, the tailors, contributed from their meager earnings to the support of their *Tzadik*, who often lived in luxury. In return for their devotion, the *Tzadik* would pray to God for them and hand out remedies for their ailments.

It was the *Tzadik*, in many cases, who was important, and not the cobbler, the weaver, the tailor. *Ḥasidism* became the worship of the *Tzadik* rather than the worship of God. No longer was it the ordinary man who came close to God, but the *Tzadik*, who prayed for him. In the minds of its opponents, *Ḥasidism* was therefore contrary to the Jewish teachings that there were no intermediaries between man and God, but that each man must pray for himself.

The Mitnagdim

There were many Jews who felt that *Ḥasidism* was a dangerous movement, that it was making prayer more important than the study of the Torah. They feared too that if *Ḥasidism* continued to spread, many teachings of Judaism would be lost. For if people believed that the prayer of the *Tzadik* had more power with God than their prayers, what would happen to the teachings of Judaism which said that all men were equal in the sight of God? This the Baal Shem Tov too had taught. But movements often change after their founders are gone. Ideas which the first teachers never dreamed of creep in. And so it was with Ḥasidism.

The people who tried to stop the spread of Ḥasidism called themselves *Mitnagdim*, which means opponents.

In the north of Poland, and especially in Lithuania, where learning was still strong, there were not as many Ḥasidim as in the south, where the need for Ḥasidism was greater. It was therefore in the north that the *Mitnagdim* were most numerous.

Rabbis denounced the movement from their pulpits. They forbade their congregations to have anything to do with the Ḥasidim. Still the tide of Ḥasidism swept on, through the towns and hamlets of Poland. It was not till a peace-loving scholar spoke from the city of Vilna, that the tide was finally stemmed.

The Scholar of Vilna

Elijah, the son of Rabbi Solomon, lived in Vilna, the "Jerusalem of Lithuania," a city of great learning, of schools and synagogues and academies. In this city, where being a scholar was considered nothing unusual, Elijah was honored as the greatest of all scholars. People called him *Gaon*, Excellency, the title they had formerly given to the leaders of the famous academies in Babylonia. Though the people of Vilna wanted him to be their

**ELIJAH
THE GAON OF VILNA**

rabbi, Elijah refused, for he wanted no public position. He preferred the quiet of his study, where he sat over his books, the Bible, the Talmud, the writings of the rabbis, mathematics, astronomy. From this quiet study, which no noise penetrated, the fame of Elijah went forth, over Vilna, over Lithuania, over all of Europe. When Elijah uttered an opinion, the people accepted it as law, so much did they honor the Gaon of Vilna.

Even as a child, Elijah had astonished the scholars of Vilna with the brilliance of his mind. By the time he reached manhood, he was looked upon as the authority on Jewish learning and Jewish law. When Elijah was forty years old, he gathered a few students about him and taught them his method of study. His method was to read and reread a passage until he understood it. He taught his students not to accept blindly the explanations of others, even of the greatest scholars. They must go back to the original, studying it till they understood it, clearly and simply, without reading into the text ideas that were not there.

Studying a Passage

It happened one day, that a messenger came running into the synagogue where Elijah's favorite pupil, Rabbi Hayyim, sat studying. Elijah wanted him at once, the messenger said. The *Gaon* was sick, and he wanted Rabbi Hayyim to come to him.

Rabbi Hayyim rushed off to Elijah's house. In hushed tones, Elijah's wife spoke to Rabbi Hayyim. Elijah had not eaten for three days, she said, because he could not understand a passage in the Talmud. For three days and nights he had been seeking the meaning, refusing to eat till he found it.

Rabbi Hayyim found Elijah in bed, his face pale and drawn, an open Talmud on his knees. "Two heads are better than one," said Elijah. And two heads bent over the page of the Talmud, seeking the meaning of the passage. Master and pupil together, they read and reread the Hebrew words in the quiet room where the blinds were drawn to shut out the movements on the street. At last they found it. Elijah rose from his bed, his illness forgotten.

A Word From Elijah

The people revered Elijah not only for his scholarliness, but for his kindness and saintliness as well. There were times when he sold his furniture to provide money for some poor family. It happened once, that the officers of the community decided that no one was to be permitted to go to private individuals to ask for money. Those who were in need were to come to a central place, where they would be given money by the officers in charge of public funds.

But a word from Elijah was enough to change the decision. Elijah understood the embarrassment some people might feel if they were forced to ask for money publicly. He therefore asked the officers to hand over a sum of money to him. This money he distributed himself to people who, he felt, should be spared the embarrassment of coming to the officers of the community.

Stopping the Tide

Yet the scholar of Vilna, whom the people called saint as well as *Gaon*, could also be moved to great wrath. He saw the rush of *Hasidism* over Poland. It had even penetrated Lithuania, and there were groups of *Hasidim* in Vilna, the seat of learning. Elijah, like other *Mitnagdim*, feared that learning would be destroyed. He too condemned the role of the *Tzadik* among the *Hasidim*, for he believed that each man was his own ambassador to God.

So Elijah uttered a ban of excommunication against the *Hasidim*. They were to be cut off from the Jewish community, he said, till they changed their ways, for their ideas were strange to Judaism.

More than anyone else, Elijah halted the spread of *Hasidism*. But this did not mean the end of the move-

The Rise of Ḥasidism

ment. The struggle between *Ḥasidim* and *Mitnagdim* went on for many years. Gradually, however, both sides came to see that they could live together. They realized that their goal was the same, the knowledge of God, though each took a different path to reach it.

BETROTHAL RING AND PERFUME BOX

(POLAND, 17th CEN.)

For the Pupil

THINGS TO READ:

1. Kalischer, Betty, *Watchmen of the Night*, "The Man of the Great Name," page 136.
2. Levin, Meyer, *The Golden Mountain*, Jonathan Cape, New York, 1932. This is a book of stories about the Baal Shem Tov.
3. Levinger, Elma, *Great Jews Since Bible Times*, "The Boy Who Became Master of the Name," page 112, and "The Joy of the Torah," page 108.

4. Lurie, Rose, *The Great March,* "Troubles Away," page 57.
5. Pessin, Deborah, *Giants on the Earth,* "The Man of Wonders," page 44, and "The Saintly Scholar," page 53.

THINGS TO TALK ABOUT:

1. There are many stories about the Baal Shem Tov. Be sure to read some of them in *The Golden Mountain.* Discuss the stories in class. Why did the Hasidim like to believe that their master had **supernatural** power?
2. Discuss the chief **differences** between the Hasidim and the Mitnagdim.

THINGS TO DO:

1. Do some illustrations for the Baal Shem Tov stories you have read.
2. Ask your father or grandfather to take you to visit a Hasidic synagogue. If possible, go on *Simhat Torah.*

Teacher's Bibliography

Buber, Martin, *Tales of the Hasidim: The Early Masters,* Schocken Books, 1947.

Ginzberg, Louis, *Students, Scholars and Saints,* "The Gaon, Rabbi Elijah of Vilna," pp. 125-144.

Grayzel, Solomon, *A History of the Jews,* pp. 521-533.

Learsi, Rufus, *Israel,* 380-386.

Margolis and Marx, *History of the Jewish People,* 578-588.

Minkin, Jacob S., *The Romance of Hasidism,* Macmillan, New York, 1935.

UNIT THREE

Leaving the Ghettos

When the Jews of Germany finally emerged from the imprisonment of the ghettos, it was as though they were seeing sunlight for the first time. So bright was the light that shone upon them, that their eyes were dazzled, and for a long time things around them seemed blurred and unreal. Confusedly, they groped about, trying to adjust themselves to the wide world they had suddenly come upon. Out of the confusion and the groping, ideas were hammered out that have affected Judaism to this day.

CHAPTER ONE

∿∿ Opening the Ghetto Gates

The People of the Ghetto

For hundreds of years the Jews of the Germanic lands had been caged up in ghettos. They had lived from generation to generation in the narrow, sunless streets called *Judengasse*, or Jews Street. These prisoners of the ghettos had been among the first settlers of the Germanic lands. They had come with the Roman conquerors and had helped build the civilization of the lands in which they had settled.

But as Christianity spread, the Church grew strong, demanding that all people join its ranks. The Jews, refusing to abandon their religion, were gradually deprived of their freedom. They were forced out of agriculture and the crafts and the professions. They were taxed into poverty and forced to wear badges to distinguish them from the Christians. They were forbidden to live anywhere but in the section of the city called the ghetto, shut away from the world they had helped to build.

Centuries went by. Weary of beating against the ghetto walls for the freedom they had lost, they finally turned their backs on the people who had scorned and oppressed them. New ideas were born in the world outside the ghetto. New books were written. But the Jews studied only their own books, the Bible and the Talmud. The language of the outside world changed, as all languages change as time goes by. Early German developed into the German that is spoken today. But the Jews spoke only the early German they had taken into the ghetto. To

Opening the Ghetto Gates

this early German they had added Hebrew words and phrases, and the language became known as Yiddish.

In the crowded ghetto, where it seemed always twilight, children grew up and married and sent their children to *Ḥeder,* as they had been sent by their parents. They continued to observe all the customs that had come down to them. They lived strictly by the Religious Code, the *Shulḥan Arukh,* which Joseph Karo had compiled in the sixteenth century. Karo was a Spanish Jew, and in gathering the laws, he had followed the customs of the Jews of Spain. A scholar of Poland, Moses Isserles, had taken the *Shulḥan Arukh* and adapted it for the majority of the Jews of Europe, whose customs were different from those of the Jews of Spain. Since the days of Isserles, the Jews of the Germanic lands had clung to the laws of the *Shulḥan Arukh* as though these alone could save them from being lost in a hostile world. The ideas of the outside world did not penetrate the ghetto walls. In the *Judengasse,* time stood still. Judaism, which had grown and blossomed through many ages, remained unchanged within the narrow ghettos.

Voices for Freedom

In the meantime, changes were taking place in the outside world. The spirit of freedom that had moved through Europe, the spirit of the Renaissance, had not died. Men who had dared to speak freely had often been killed. But the longing for freedom had grown stronger.

Years passed. The sixteenth century rolled into the seventeenth. Kings and emperors still ruled by what they considered "divine right." Peasants still toiled on land that was not theirs. Filled with hatred because of their poverty, many people might have risen against the kings and noblemen for whom they toiled. But their oppressors persuaded them that it was because of the Jews that they were poor. And so they turned their hatred against the Jews.

It was easy for them to hate the Jews, who were shut up in their ghettos. They did not know the inner life of the Jews, and their ideals of brotherhood and justice. The people with the yellow badges and the queer hats meant, to the Christians, Jews. More than this they did not know. They had been told for hundreds of years that the Jews were a "strange" people with "queer" customs, a people who must be shunned.

But a day was to come, toward the end of the eighteenth century, when the people of America would proclaim that all men were created equal.

A day was to come, not long after the American revo-

JEWISH WEDDING IN 18th CENTURY GERMANY * THE BRIDE IS VEILED

BRIDE AND GROOM UNDER THE HUPPAH (MARRIAGE CANOPY)

lution, when the people of France would throw off their kings and noblemen and proclaim liberty, equality and fraternity for all men.

But in the meantime, there was still oppression. Here and there, however, always growing louder, voices were raised for freedom.

The Voice of Lessing

In Prussia, which was one of the Germanic lands, there lived a young man called Gotthold Ephraim Lessing. Lessing, who was a Christian, wanted the emancipation, or freedom, of the Jews. He believed that no people should be denied their rights because of difference of religion. It was a blot on his own people, thought Lessing, to deny freedom to the Jews.

Like most Germans, Lessing did not know any Jews, though there were many of them in the ghettos of his land. But he saw no reason why Jews should be considered any different from Christians. To tear away the prejudice which blinded the eyes of his people, he wrote a play called *The Jews*. In this play Lessing made his hero a Jew, and had him save the life of a baron. When the baron wished to reward him, the Jew refused to accept anything, even the hand of the baron's daughter. Amazed at his rescuer's refusal to marry the beautiful maiden, the baron demanded the reason. "I am a Jew," the Jew replied. The baron, who had never met a Jew, was stupefied. He had never dreamt that a Jew could be generous and noble. "If all Jews were like you," he exclaimed, "how we would respect them!" "If all Christians were like you," said the Jew, "how lovable they would be!"

Lessing's play was attacked by the critics who, like the baron, did not know any Jews. There were no Jews like the Jew in Lessing's play, they said. It was impossible, they insisted, for a Jew to be noble.

Several years later Lessing met a Jew in the city of Berlin. They sat over a game of chess, Jew and Christian, and played and chatted. This was very strange in Berlin, for such a thing was never seen. And Lessing realized that he had been right and not the critics. Here was a Jew like the hero of his play. His name was Moses Mendelssohn.

Moses Mendelssohn

Moses Mendelssohn came to Berlin from Dessau when he was a boy of fourteen. He came alone, trudging along the road for five days, for Dessau was eighty miles from Berlin. He came because he wanted to be with his teacher,

Rabbi David Fraenkel, who had been called away from Dessau to be Chief Rabbi of Berlin. Moses loved his teacher, who had taught him the Bible and the Talmud, and had introduced him to the books of Maimonides. When Rabbi Fraenkel was gone, there was no one in Dessau who could teach him, and several months later the lad set out to find his teacher. Moses' father could give him no money to take the trip in comfort, for he was a poor scribe who made a living by writing out copies of the Torah. So Moses came to Berlin with only a few coppers in his pockets.

Berlin had a special gate through which Jews entered. It was called Jews Gate, and at it stood a watchman. To his dismay, Moses found that not every Jew could enter Berlin. Only a handful of rich Jews and their employees could live in the city, and certainly no one who could not earn a living. Moses told the watchman that he was a student of Rabbi Fraenkel, who was Chief Rabbi of the Jews in the city, and that he had come to continue his studies with him. Moses paid the toll to the watchman, and entered the city.

The Student

Rabbi Fraenkel did all he could to help the boy who had walked all the way to Berlin to be with him. He employed him to copy a commentary he was writing on the Jerusalem Talmud, and asked a friend to give him a bed in the attic of his house. With the few pennies Moses earned each week, he would buy a loaf of bread, which he divided into equal parts. He forced himself to eat no more than one portion of the loaf of bread each day, for if he ate two, his supply would run out before he could buy another loaf. Often he went to bed hungry, yet he was happy. He was with his teacher, for whom he had wept on the hill outside of Dessau as he watched him disappear in the distance.

In his garret room, where he spent all his leisure time at his books, Moses studied the literature of the Jews. But soon he learned of other books of which his people did not know.

Moses Mendelssohn wanted the culture of the world outside the ghetto walls. He met a Polish schoolmaster who taught him mathematics. A Jewish physician taught him Latin. He studied French and German. He read the philosophy of the great thinkers of Europe. In his attic room, he sat day and night over his precious books.

Seven years went by. Moses Mendelssohn was twenty-one years old when he became the tutor of the children of a rich manufacturer. Four years later, he became his employer's bookkeeper, and finally, his partner. But Moses Mendelssohn continued to study. His studies gave him wisdom and nobility, and they showed him the world from which his people had been barred.

The Friends

Then Mendelssohn met Lessing. As men often do who have no prejudices, they discovered that despite their different religions, they liked each other. Mendelssohn had found a lovable Christian, and Lessing had found a Jew he could respect.

Through Lessing, Mendelssohn met other Christians, and his home became a meeting place for German men of culture. Mendelssohn was shy at first, for he had known only the ghetto. But Lessing helped to draw him out. He encouraged his Jewish friend to write out the philosophical ideas he often discussed, and Mendelssohn began to write, in the German language. First there were articles, which Lessing sent to a magazine to be published. Gradually, the name Mendelssohn came to be known in all the Germanic lands. In time he wrote a book of philosophy, and Mendelssohn, a son of a despised people, became famous throughout Europe for the beauty of his German and the nobility of his thinking.

Still determined to destroy prejudice and help break down the ghetto walls, Lessing wrote another play,

Nathan the Wise. Again the hero, Nathan, was a noble Jew. But this time the critics could not say that such a Jew was impossible. For all the world knew that Lessing's model for Nathan was Moses Mendelssohn, the sage of Berlin.

Helping His People

While Lessing and other Christians tried to break down the ghetto walls from without, Mendelssohn worked from within. He would teach his people, he thought, that they could remain faithful to their own religion, as he was, and still enjoy the culture of the outside world. But first they must learn German, the language of the country.

To help them learn German, Mendelssohn translated the Five Books of Moses and the Book of Psalms into the language of the land. He used the Hebrew characters, or letters, in his translation, for the Jews could not read German. To bring them the culture of other peoples, he encouraged a group of Jewish scholars to publish a magazine, *Ha-Me'assef, The Gatherer.* The articles in the magazine, written in Hebrew, gathered for their readers many of the ideas in the world outside the ghetto. Some of Mendelssohn's wealthy Jewish friends also opened a school for children. Not only were the Hebrew subjects taught at this school, but also the German language.

Mendelssohn became a symbol, both for the Jews and for the Christians. For the Christians he was the symbol of what the Jews could become if the rights of which they had been deprived were restored to them. For the young Jewish men and women of the ghettos he became the symbol of what they must do in order to become emancipated. They believed that if they learned German and studied western culture, they too, like Mendelssohn, would be accepted by the outside world.

And while the young people in the ghetto studied the translations he had written for them, dreaming of emancipation, the eighteenth century went rolling on.

For the Pupil

THINGS TO READ:

1. Kalischer, Betty, *Watchmen of the Night,* "The Third Moses," page 147.
2. Levinger, Elma, *Great Jews Since Bible Times,* "To Seek His Fortune," page 117.
3. Pessin, Deborah, *Giants on the Earth,* "The Man Who Broke the Ghetto Walls," page 58, and "The House of the Red Shield," page 68.

THINGS TO TALK ABOUT:

1. Why did time stand still in the ghettos?
2. Why did Lessing believe that denying the Jews their rights was a blot on his own people?
3. Why did Mendelssohn believe that a translation of the Bible into German would help introduce the Jews to the outside world?

THINGS TO DO:

1. Pretend you are Moses Mendelssohn and you have just arrived in Berlin. Write a letter to your father telling him about your journey and how you are living in Berlin.

2. Do some research on the ghettos in the Germanic lands. Your teacher or the librarian will show you how to go about it. When your research is done, discuss ghetto life with your classmates. You may like to do a few pictures portraying ghetto life. Show the homes, the costumes, the occupations.

Teacher's Bibliography

Abrahams, Israel, *Jewish Life in the Middle Ages,* Jewish Publication Society, 1911.

Grayzel, Solomon, *A History of the Jews,* pp. 473-489; 534-548.

Learsi, Rufus, *Israel,* pp. 386-390.

Lowenthal, Marvin, *The Jews of Germany,* Jewish Publication Society, 1936.

The Memoirs of Gluckel of Hameln, translated by Marvin Lowenthal, Behrman House, 1932.

Margolis and Marx, *History of the Jewish People,* pp. 589-599.

Walter, H., *Moses Mendelssohn,* Bloch Publishing Co., 1930.

CHAPTER TWO

ᨆ Entering the Outside World

The French Revolution

In the year 1789, three years after Mendelssohn's death, Europe was shaken by a cry that came out of France: "Liberty, Equality, Fraternity!" The people of France had risen against their king and noblemen and overthrown them. They had proclaimed freedom from tyranny and equality for all.

For a number of years there was great confusion in France. The monarchy was gone, and the people were inexperienced in any other kind of government. In the neighboring lands, kings still reigned. In America alone was there a republic. And though America was far away, her example of freedom, shining like a great light across the ocean, guided the people of France in forming their own republic.

In the year 1792, France proclaimed herself a republic. Several months later, King Louis XVI, accused of conspiring with enemies of the republic to bring back the monarchy, was executed.

The kings of other European lands feared the new republic. When France sneezes, someone has said, all of Europe catches cold. What happened in France, thought the monarchs of Europe, might also happen in their own lands. For could not the French republic become an example for their own people to follow?

A mighty alliance of many nations was formed. The armies of Europe marched toward France. But the enthusiasm of the ragged French soldiers was far stronger than the alliance of foreign armies. They marched across their borders into Holland, sweeping the allied forces before them.

The Fall of the Ghettos

Wherever they came, the French demanded an end of the old order of oppression and tyranny. Jews had been living comfortably in Holland for many years, but with the coming of the French they were given a right they had never enjoyed, the right of citizenship.

When Napoleon Bonaparte took over the leadership of the French army, all of Europe was swept along in the tide of the French Revolution. Napoleon marched into Italy, and though he shared the popular prejudice against the Jews, the slogan of the revolution became the order of the day. Liberty, equality, fraternity! The Jews tore off their yellow badges and streamed out of the ghettos of Venice, Livorno, Rome. The gates of the ghettos went up in flames.

Several years later freedom came for the Jews in the Germanic cities and states. The nearer to France, the more rights the Jews won. In Westphalia, Lubeck, Bremen, they were given full citizenship. In some places the German rulers were forced to give the Jews rights at

OUTSIDE THE GHETTO WALLS

the point of the sword. "All traces of slavery are abolished. . . ." proclaimed the French commissioner at Cologne. "You shall account to God alone for your religion . . . all men are equal before the law."

With the coming of the French, Jews were permitted to live in Cologne. In many places, like Frankfort, they paid for their freedom with money. In Prussia, they were given their freedom so that they would help fight the French armies invading the land.

EUROPE
AND THE CONGRESS OF VIENNA

The Return of Tyranny

In 1815, Napoleon was defeated at Waterloo. Again the tide turned, this time in favor of monarchy. The kings of Europe met in Vienna to decide how to restore what the revolution had swept away. The Jews of the Germanic lands sent their spokesmen to the meetings in Vienna, hoping to save some of the rights they had won. They had tasted freedom. They had sent their sons to the universities. They had moved about like free men in the outside world. And they did not want to return to the ghettos and the yellow badges.

The new rulers of the Germanic lands tried to remove every trace of freedom which the Revolution had brought. Revolts among the peasants were crushed. In many places, the Jews were forced into the ghettos again, although, loyal to their native lands, they had fought against the French armies. Unable to vent their rage against the French, who had defeated them, many Germans attacked the Jews, for they were nearer and easier victims. Germany must be united and strong, said many Germans. The Jews, they claimed, were not Germans. They were a "strange" people within the land. And again, as often before, many Jews were robbed, beaten, killed.

The Easier Path

Since the days of Mendelssohn, who had been honored by Jews and Christians alike, the younger generation of

Jews had longed for emancipation. Mendelssohn had been their father, their guiding star. Eagerly, they had studied German, hoping it would be their passport into the civilization of the outside world. They wanted to attend the universities. They wanted to enter the professions. They wanted the freedom to enjoy life.

The French Revolution had brought emancipation closer. The Jews had streamed out of the ghettos. Many of them had entered the universities. They had studied the professions. They had hoped to be welcomed by the outside world. But the restoration of the monarchy had crushed their hopes.

There was no return, they felt, to the old way of life they had left behind. And the people whose equals they had hoped to be, had met them with scorn. They felt lost between two worlds, the world they had left and the world that refused them entrance. What must they do, they asked themselves, to win the freedom that had been dangled before them for so short a time?

Many Jews decided that being Jewish was too difficult. Some left Judaism eagerly. Some reluctantly abandoned their religion and adopted Christianity. The part-

Entering the Outside World

ing from the faith of their fathers was not always easy, for the ties that bound them to their people were strong. Yet they accepted baptism, for it brought them new opportunities and freedom. Even the children of Mendelssohn, who had been a religious Jew, turned to Christianity.

The leaders of Judaism in Germany saw with dismay what was happening in their ranks. They saw the rush of many of their men and women to the altars of the church. They knew that there had been crises for the Jews many times before. And always, they had found a way of meeting them. They were confident that now too they would find a way.

For the Pupil

THINGS TO TALK ABOUT:

1. Many people believe that Moses Mendelssohn did more harm than good when he tried to lead the Jews into the outside world. What do you think?
2. Why did many Jews feel lost between two worlds when oppression returned to the Germanic lands?

THINGS TO DO:

Heinrich Heine, a German Jewish poet, accepted baptism though he remained loyal to Judaism in his heart. Many of Heinrich Heine's poems are on Jewish subjects. Ask your school librarian, or the librarian in your public library, to help you find some English translations of Heine's poems which deal with Jewish subjects.

ᾝᾝ Teacher's Bibliography

Grayzel, Solomon, *A History of the Jews*, pp. 570-582.
Learsi, Rufus, *Israel*, pp. 401-421.
Margolis and Marx, *History of the Jewish People*, pp. 608-626.

SYNAGOGUE IN BERLIN OF THE TIME OF MENDELSSOHN

CHAPTER THREE

Three Ways of Judaism

The Reform Movement

The synagogue had always been the center of Jewish life. The Jews came to the synagogue to study as well as to pray. They came to discuss social matters, and the news of the day. In the Middle Ages, a man had the right to rise and interrupt the prayers if he had a grievance against his neighbor, for the synagogue was also a house of justice. Travelers came to the synagogue for shelter, and the poor came for help. Family celebrations were often held in the synagogue, and on Purim and *Simhat Torah* the walls re-echoed with the sound of merry voices. The synagogue bubbled with life. To the Jews of the ghetto the synagogue was home.

As many Jews forsook the synagogues for the churches, a movement began to beautify and modernize the services of the synagogue, so that the young people would find it more attractive. The leaders of this movement, which was called Reform, wanted to introduce into the synagogue the dignity and solemnity of the church, which was used only as a house of worship. By making the atmosphere of the synagogue more like that of the church, they hoped to keep their people faithful to their own religion.

In the province of Westphalia, Israel Jacobson, an important Jewish leader, introduced several changes in the synagogue services. A weekly sermon was delivered by the rabbi in the German language. Several of the prayers were recited in German rather than in Hebrew, for many people no longer understood Hebrew. A choir of men and women sang songs in German, and instrumental music played softly as the worshippers chanted their prayers.

Slowly the idea of change in the synagogue services spread. A new house of worship was opened in Hamburg. This house of worship was called a temple rather than a synagogue, for to the followers of Reform Judaism the name synagogue was connected with the dreary life of the ghetto. Organ music played in the temple of Hamburg. A choir sang. Rabbis delivered sermons in German. Prayers were recited in German, the language of the land.

Then more drastic changes were introduced by the leaders of the Reform movement. They broke with many customs and laws found in the *Shulḥan Arukh*, believing they were no longer necessary. And in the prayers, the passages expressing the hope of a Messiah and a return to Zion were removed. The Jews were constantly being attacked as "foreigners," as people who could never become loyal German citizens. The Reform leaders hoped that by removing from the prayers all references to Zion, their critics would be silenced. In the Germanic lands, they said, the Jews were Germans, and they no longer wished to return to Palestine, the land of their forefathers.

Conflict Among the Jews

The changes brought a storm of protest against the Reform movement. The Orthodox Jews, who followed every rule in the *Shulḥan Arukh,* every custom which had come down to them, protested most violently against the changes introduced by the leaders of the Reform. They believed that every Jewish custom and law was sacred and must remain unchanged for all time to come.

But the protests did not halt the progress of the Reform movement. It grew stronger and bolder. A temple was opened in Leipzig, the city where the famous German fairs were held, and where many Jews came twice each year to attend these fairs. Services were held in the Leipzig temple, and the people who attended them returned home with new ideas for their communities. Temples were opened in other cities, and even in other lands, in France and in America.

In the meantime, the storm roused by the Reform movement grew more violent. But in its violence, opinions grew clearer as men spoke their minds. And Jewish leaders brought their ideas before the people.

A Champion of Orthodox Judaism

A man now came forward, Rabbi Samson Raphael Hirsch, to state what he and all Orthodox Jews believed to be the truth about Judaism. The Torah, said Hirsch, was given to the people by God on Mount Sinai. The *Shulḥan Arukh* expressed the laws contained in the

·ZECHARIAH FRANKEL·   ·ABRAHAM GEIGER·

Torah. Therefore it was holy and must in no way be changed. For who was man to challenge the wisdom of God, or to alter what God had given? The Jews must accept as sacred all their laws and customs.

There was no conflict for the Jews, said Hirsch, between being Orthodox and being citizens of the lands in which they lived. The Jews had an ideal to hand on to mankind, the ideal of brotherhood under God. To keep this ideal alive, they must remain Jews, loyal to every custom of their people. They might find it difficult at times to observe the customs of their fathers. But this did not matter. For a people with a mission could not always live a life of ease and comfort. They must sometimes expect discomfort, and even hardship.

A Champion of Reform Judaism

"Judaism is not a finished tale!" said Abraham Geiger, the champion of the Reform movement. Like all living things, its form must sometimes change. Each generation of Jews must study Judaism and find its meaning and its spirit. Each generation must find the form that will express this spirit best. And each generation must develop its own idea of Judaism. The customs that suited our forefathers are not necessarily the customs for us. Our forefathers understood and spoke Hebrew, and the prayers had meaning for them. If the people no longer understand Hebrew, then the prayers must be translated into a language they understand. In a changing world, we too must change, or Judaism will cease to have meaning.

Champion of Continuity

There is some truth, said Zechariah Frankel, the champion of Historical Judaism, in what the Orthodox Jews believe, and some truth in what the Reform Jews believe. Judaism, he agreed, is not dead. It is alive, and like all living things, it grows and changes. But though change is introduced, the continuity of our history must not be broken. As Judaism has changed in the past, so will it change in the future. As prayer took the place of sacrifice, so other changes will take place.

But when we make our changes, we must make them cautiously, without breaking with our past. Jewish life must go on and on, without breaks, so that what was developed in the past will not be lost. We must not destroy the past in order to preserve Judaism, but we must cautiously change only the customs that will help its growth. Change must take place only in continuity.

There are certain customs and ideas, however, that are basic in Judaism—Hebrew, as the language of prayer, the hope of a Messiah and a return to Zion. These are so deeply implanted in the hearts of the Jews, that they cannot be uprooted. These ideas must therefore remain unchanged.

The point of view expressed by Zechariah Frankel was called Historical Judaism. It became, in time, the basis of what is known today as Conservative Judaism.

The Science of Judaism

As the religious leaders were trying to draw the people closer to Judaism through religion, other leaders showed them another path to the same goal. This path was the path of knowledge.

"Know thyself," these leaders said. For they felt that if the Jews knew their history and their great achievements, their pride in their past would keep them loyal to their own religion.

But the past was buried in mist. There was no record of what had happened during the many centuries when the Jews had been shut away from the world. There were no history books to tell them who their heroes were, what they had achieved, when they had lived. They had the Bible, the Talmud, the prayers, and many other great works written by their rabbis and scholars. They had old documents which no one read. And that was all.

Three Ways of Judaism

Portraits: Leopold Zunz and Heinrich Graetz

Then a man called Leopold Zunz opened the gateway to Jewish history. And a man called Heinrich Graetz entered the gate that Zunz had opened.

Leopold Zunz

Leopold Zunz lived through most of the nineteenth century. He was born in 1794 and lived for ninety-two years. Most of his long life Leopold Zunz spent in trying to bring to the Jews a knowledge of their past, so that their pride might be re-awakened.

Zunz began his studies in the manner of most Jewish boys. He studied Hebrew, the Bible and the Talmud. But soon he went on to other studies, and finally he entered the University of Berlin. Here he learned how to study a subject scientifically, by examining old records and picking out the important facts, then putting the facts together so that they formed a complete picture.

Zunz called the scientific study of the Jewish past the Science of Judaism. And like a scientist, he studied all the records he could gather to see what facts he could find.

One of Zunz's most important works was his history of Jewish prayers. He spent fifty years on this work, searching museums, libraries and synagogues for old manuscripts and records. He went hundreds of miles for a single sentence.

Zunz discovered, in the Jewish prayers, a record of Jewish heroism and martyrdom. Prayers had often been composed for men and women who had died for their religion, and in these prayers, Zunz found the pain of oppression and ghetto life, and the longing for peace and freedom. When his work was finished, it brought to light a long, dark period of Jewish history which stretched over hundreds of years.

Heinrich Graetz

Following in the footsteps of Leopold Zunz, came a young Jewish scholar, Heinrich Graetz. His purpose, too, was to bring to the Jews a knowledge of themselves. To bring them this knowledge, he undertook the great task of writing the history of the Jewish people. Like Zunz, Graetz plowed through thousands of old records, seeking the facts, then arranging them into the great panorama of Jewish history. The work took many years, but at last the Jews had the first complete history of their people. They were now able to read the heroic story of Israel from the dim Biblical past to their own day in the Germanic lands. And many Jews were able to regain the pride and self-confidence they had lost in the ghettos.

In Later Germany

As the Jews emerged more and more from the ghettos and tried to adjust themselves to the life about them, the struggle for complete emancipation went on. Now it seemed distant, now close at hand, depending upon the conditions in the land.

The emancipation of the Jews went hand in hand with the growth of freedom among the general population. The more rights the general population won, the closer came the complete emancipation of the Jews.

Europe did not long remain quiet after the fall of Napoleon and the return of the monarchy. For the craving for freedom could not be crushed. Time and again as the years passed, Europe shook with revolution. Though uprisings were often crushed, monarchs trembled on their thrones, for they feared the end of their power. The greater their fear, the more cruelly did they crush the revolts in their lands.

The year 1848 was a year of rebellion in many of the European lands. Among the revolutionaries who fought and died in the uprisings, there were thousands of Jews. They fought not only for their own emancipation, but for the emancipation of all the people.

For years the struggle went on, while the forces for freedom grew stronger. In the meantime, the demand for unity of the Germanic states also grew stronger. Finally, the Germanic states were united into a single land, Germany. In the year 1871, a united Germany adopted a liberal constitution granting full rights to all its citizens, regardless of their religion.

The constitution brought complete emancipation to the Jews of Germany. All their hopes and dreams of freedom had at last been realized. Again they were free men in a free world.

For the Pupil

THINGS TO TALK ABOUT:

1. How did the Reform movement try to adjust Judaism to modern times?
2. Why did Historical, or Conservative Judaism, oppose Reform Judaism?
3. What is meant by "change in continuity"?
4. How did Leopold Zunz and Heinrich Graetz open the gateway to the past?

Teacher's Bibliography

Grayzel, Solomon, *A History of the Jews*, pp. 583-599.

Learsi, Rufus, *Israel*, pp. 421-431.

Margolis and Marx, *History of the Jewish People*, pp. 632-641.

UNIT FOUR

In the Land of the Czars

THE BRUTALITY of the Czars of Russia set the Jews of that country moving in two directions. It was late in the nineteenth century that the movement began, when thousands upon thousands of Jews fled the land of the Czars. Most of the Jews went west, to America, Land of the Free. Some went east, to Palestine, Land of Memories. In both lands the Jews built strong communities, because in both lands they were free.

CHAPTER ONE

∿∿ Oppression Under Czarism

The Slumbering East

East of the lands of Western Europe, a giant country, Russia, sprawled. In this land of endless plains and forestland, change came slowly and late, as though the ideas of the West found it difficult to make their way across the windy, frozen steppes. While industries developed in the western countries and revolutions brought changes in government, Russia slumbered on in the feudal past. Serfs lived in primitive huts clustered together in untidy villages. Overlooking the villages were the estates of the noblemen, who lived in idleness and luxury. Hand in hand with Russia's backwardness went ignorance and superstition.

The rulers of this vast feudal country were the Czars, whose policy it was to keep Jews from settling in Russia. Despite the unfriendliness of the Czars, however, Russia was to become the home of millions of Jews. In 1654, Russia took over the Ukraine, making it part of her territory. Elizabeth, Czarina of Russia, permitted the Jews to remain where they were, in the villages of the Ukraine. But they were permitted to dwell in no other part of Russia. More than a hundred years later, Poland was partitioned by Russia, Austria and Prussia. To Russia fell that part of Poland where almost a million Jews lived. Whether they liked it or not, the Czars now had many Jews as their subjects.

"Except Jews"

Catherine II, who was Czarina of Russia when Poland was partitioned, followed the example of Elizabeth. She permitted the Jews to live only in the section of land which had been part of Poland, excluding them from the rest of Russia. This section, stretching along the western border of Russia, was called the Pale of Settlement. But even within the Pale, Jews could not live wherever they pleased. They could live only in towns and villages specified by the government.

Yet Catherine liked to think of herself as a liberal ruler. She spoke of liberty, hoping that words would take the place of deeds. She promised religious freedom to the people of Poland who were now under her rule. Catherine permitted the Jews their *Kahals,* as they had existed in Poland, except that now the *Kahals* were to be merely for collecting taxes, both for the Russian government and for their own needs.

The poverty-stricken serfs of Russia had few rights. But the Jews had even less. They had nothing except what the law specifically said they might have. When a few rights were grudgingly granted to the people, they were granted to everyone, "except Jews."

The Reign of Alexander

By the time Catherine ended her reign, in 1796, the ideas of the French Revolution had taken hold in the minds of many Russians. People began to talk of reforms and constitutions and freedom for the serfs.

Alexander I, who was Czar after Paul, the son of Catherine, knew that he could not shut Russia off from the West. Nor could he stop the people from thinking of reforms and a more liberal government. Wishing his subjects to look upon him as kind and just, he promised them greater freedom.

Like the Czars before him, however, Alexander regarded the Jews as a "strange" people. They spoke their own language, Yiddish, instead of Russian. They clung to their own religion, their own books, their own schools. Russia's schools and universities had always been closed to the Jews. But Alexander, eager to wipe out the differences between Jews and Christians, declared that the Russian schools were now open to them. They might open their own schools as well, if they liked, provided that the language of these schools be Russian, Polish or German.

The Jews of Russia had always been forbidden to own land, so that there were practically no farmers among them. To earn a living, Jews usually practiced handicrafts—tailoring or cobbling. Or they ran taverns, or small stores where the peasants came to buy their supplies. Seeing that Jews were not farmers, Alexander called them "unproductive." He would force them, he decided, to become good Russian farmers.

To do this, Alexander added two new sections to the Pale of Settlement, Astrakhan and the Caucasus. And he issued a decree stating that by January, 1808, the villages of the Pale of Settlement were to be cleared of Jews, who were to turn to the soil for a livelihood.

As the date of expulsion drew near, the Jews of the

Pale became panic-stricken. Alexander's "kindness" had turned into a nightmare. They had been living in the villages of the Pale for many years. They had no knowledge of farming, no equipment, no way of getting to Astrakhan and the Caucasus. And if they did get there, who was to help them learn farming?

But almost at the last moment, Alexander's edict was suspended. Napoleon's armies were marching toward Russia. Fearing that the Jews might welcome Napoleon as their liberator, Alexander postponed the day of their expulsion. The Jews, however, to Alexander's amazement, remained loyal to Russia.

Yet when the danger of the French seemed past, Alexander's edict was carried through. Thousands of Jews were driven out of their villages into the larger towns, where they were left in the open squares. Since the towns were already crowded, it was expected that the Jews would go off and manage to become farmers. But only a few hundred families became farmers. The rest were forced into the greatest misery and poverty they had ever suffered.

In 1815 Napoleon was defeated at Waterloo. In Western Europe the monarchs tried to wipe out the reforms the French had brought to their lands. Alexander followed their example. As the demand for freedom in Russia grew stronger, Alexander turned oppressor. His early dream of being looked upon by his people as kind and just was forgotten. The few crumbs of freedom he had thrown to his people were withdrawn. In 1824, Jews were again uprooted from their homes and driven into towns. Again they were left stranded, without a roof to cover them, and with no way of earning a living.

The Iron Czar

After Alexander came his son Nicholas, the "Iron Czar" of Russia. Nicholas did not believe in kindness. He had no patience with the Jews who, it seemed to him, were a stubborn people, refusing to accept the customs of Russia. He would force them, he decided, to become Russianized. This meant, to Nicholas, becoming Christians.

Nicholas wanted the finest army in Europe. All soldiers, except Jews, began service at the age of eighteen, and the length of service was twenty-five years. Nicholas hoped that during this long period soldiers of minority groups would forget their folk customs and languages. His army would be a solid mass, its soldiers speaking the same language, observing the same religion. This was the way, thought Nicholas, of having a strong army and a united people.

Oppression Under Czarism

For the Jews, Nicholas planned for more than twenty-five years of service. They were to serve six years longer than other soldiers, beginning when they were twelve.

Cantonists

Terror swept through the Jewish villages of the Pale as boys of twelve were carted off to be turned into soldiers. They were taken to far distant cantons, or districts, thousands of miles from home. And they were trained not only to be soldiers. Nicholas wanted to turn them into Christians, even if it had to be done by force. The boys were flogged and tortured. Salted food was forced into their mouths and they were denied water to quench their thirst. Many of them died. Many of them, unable to bear

JEWISH OFFICER AND SOLDIERS IN THE POLISH NATIONAL GUARD DURING THE UPRISING AGAINST RUSSIA IN 1831

the torture, consented to be baptized. And many, despite all the tortures they suffered, refused to abandon the faith of their fathers.

At home, parents became frantic at the thought of what was happening to their sons. Since the Jews had to provide proportionately more soldiers than the rest of the population, there were often not enough twelve year old boys to conscript. The *Kahal,* however, was held responsible for supplying the required number of cantonists, as the conscripts were called. But where were they to get them? Children of ten or even eight and six were often snatched from their mothers' arms. Men called "snatchers" prowled about among the Jews, pouncing on young boys. Parents could not let their sons out of their sight. Boys ran off to the forests, where they were hunted, like wild beasts. "The snatchers are coming!" The cry would ring through the village, and the village was thrown into panic as men and women ran about in a frenzy looking for their children. As the Jewish mothers in Egypt had tried to hide their sons, hoping to save them from being drowned in the Nile River, so the Jewish mothers of Russia hid their young sons in the attics and cellars of their homes, hoping to save them from conversion.

Crown Schools

Another way, thought Nicholas, of Russianizing the Jews quickly, was by setting up special schools for them. What made the Jews a stubborn people, he believed, was their religion, their Talmud, the customs they observed. If they could be parted from these, they would become true Russians.

So Nicholas issued a decree ordering the establishment of crown, or government schools, for the Jews of Russia. Many Jews, eager to learn the culture of the outside world, went to the schools. But most of the Jews did not trust Nicholas. They suspected that the Czar's real purpose was not to open the doors of the world to them, but to turn them away from Judaism.

Nicholas's minister of education, Uvarov, felt that he must have an influential Jew to persuade the people to accept the crown schools. He looked about and decided on a man called Max Lilienthal, who was a graduate of a German university. At this time, Lilienthal was successfully conducting a modern Jewish school in Riga, and Uvarov invited him to accept the post of working with the Jews of the Pale. Lilienthal believed that the Jews of Russia should be introduced to the culture of the western world, and he traveled through the villages of the Pale, urging them to attend the crown schools. But the Jews told Lilienthal that they did not trust the Czar, that he was using the crown schools to draw them away from Judaism. Max Lilienthal could not believe this. No government, he insisted, could be so treacherous. If it turned out that the Jews were right, he would resign his post at once.

It did turn out that the Jews were right. When Lilienthal discovered to what use he had been put by the Czar, he resigned from his post, left Russia, and sailed for America. As for the crown schools, the Jews themselves had to pay for their upkeep, through taxes on meat and candles. But in the end they failed to accomplish the Czar's purpose, and during the reign of the next Czar, they were abolished.

Narrowing the Pale of Settlement

Nicholas tried still other ways of converting the Jews to Christianity. He opened several colonies for Jewish farmers in the far ends of Russia. To Jews who would settle in these colonies Nicholas promised free land and tax exemption, if they agreed to baptism. Though many Jews longed for land of their own to plow and reap, they refused to accept the terms Nicholas offered.

Enraged at the failure of all his plans, Nicholas passed edict after edict, further narrowing the Pale, driving more and more Jews from their homes in the villages. From the civilized countries came cries of protest. Sir Moses Montefiore, a famous Jewish philanthropist who lived in England, came to see the Czar, bearing with him a letter from Queen Victoria. Sir Moses was received with great honors at the palace of the Czar. His proposals for improving the conditions of his people were courteously received. Moses Montefiore returned to England, hoping he had brought relief to the Jews of Russia. But the heart of the "Iron Czar" did not soften. Nothing was done to relieve the Russian Jews of their suffering.

Hope of Liberation

Nicholas died in 1855, after warring with the Jews for thirty years. After Nicholas came Alexander II, an educated young prince who began his reign by introducing many reforms. On ascending the throne of Russia, the young Czar surrounded himself with liberal advisers. To help Russia catch up with Western Europe, Alexander decided to wipe out serfdom. He issued an edict of emancipation, freeing forty million serfs. Throughout Europe Alexander became known as the Emancipator. Hope ran high among the Russians who had demanded greater freedom. And to the Jews, hemmed in in their Pale of Settlement, it seemed that at last their day of liberation too had come.

For the Pupil

THINGS TO READ:

1. Kalischer, Betty, *Watchmen of the Night,* "The Man of Charity," page 176.
2. Levinger, Elma, *Great Jews Since Bible Times,* "In an English Garden," page 138.
3. Lurie, Rose, *The Great March,* Book Two, "He Never Stops," page 69.
4. Pessin, Deborah, *Giants on the Earth,* Part Two, "Rise, Sir Moses," page 35.
5. Steinberg, Judah, *In Those Days,* Jewish Publication Society, 1915.

THINGS TO TALK ABOUT:

1. Why were there so few farmers among the Jews of Russia?
2. Despite the force used by Alexander I and Nicholas, why did the Jews remain city dwellers instead of becoming farmers?
3. Why did the crown schools fail?

4. The "Iron Czar" thought that unity meant everyone thinking alike, worshipping alike. So did Antiochus, in the days of the Maccabees. Both kings failed to convert the Jews. Discuss the policies of the two kings and the reasons for their failure. Why is it incorrect to think that uniformity means unity?

THINGS TO DO:

Some of you probably have grandfathers who served in the armies of a Czar. Ask them to tell you what they remember about it.

Teacher's Bibliography

Eisenberg, Azriel (Editor), *Modern Jewish Life in Literature,* United Synagogue of America, 1948. Part One, "The Old World."

Grayzel, Solomon, *A History of the Jews,* pp. 600-605.

Learsi, Rufus, *Israel,* pp. 449-462.

Margolis and Marx, *History of the Jewish People,* pp. 627-631, 665-674.

MEDALLION FROM SILVER TORAH CROWN
SHOWING JACOB'S DREAM
(POLAND)

CHAPTER TWO

〰️ Enlightenment

The Gifts of a Czar

Alexander II began his reign by giving his Jewish subjects a few rights they had never enjoyed. He hoped that through greater freedom they would abandon their old way of living.

Alexander began by issuing a decree discontinuing the canton system. Henceforth, Jews were to be conscripted for the army like all others, when they were eighteen. Boys under eighteen who were already in the army, except those who had been baptized, were sent home.

Anxious to use the skill and the money of his Jewish subjects for the benefit of the country, Alexander opened the large cities to Jews with money to invest in industry, and to merchants who carried on extensive trade. Later, he extended this privilege to university graduates and to skilled mechanics and artisans.

Thus the Jews began to contribute to Russia's development. Merchants imported and exported goods. Men of wealth built railroads and exploited mines. Jews flocked to the universities to study the professions, so that they could leave the Pale and live in the cities of the interior. They became doctors, surgeons, dentists, lawyers. More and more Jews entered the universities, eager for the culture of the outside world and for the opportunities the Czar offered them.

But Alexander's kindness meant little to most of the Jews. They still feared the iron fist within the velvet glove. They feared too that Russianization of their young might lead to baptism. So most of the Jews remained where they were, living by their *Shulḥan Arukh*, as they had in the past.

Enlightenment

What had happened in Germany, in the days of Mendelssohn and after, happened in Russia. Jews who had learned the culture of the outside world tried to bring it to their people. They would lead them, they believed, out of darkness into light. They would draw them into a great and friendly Russia. These men who tried to introduce the culture of Europe to the Jews of the Pale were called *Maskilim*, and the movement for enlightenment was called *Haskalah*.

As far back as the reign of the "Iron Czar," Nicholas I, there were already men working for the enlightenment of the Jews. Isaac Baer Levinsohn, whom the people

ISAAC BAER LEVINSOHN

called the Russian Mendelssohn, urged his people to introduce new subjects into the curriculum of their schools —Hebrew grammar, Russian, the European languages. Art and science, he wrote, were progressing. To study these, the Jews must go to the books of other peoples. All through his life, Levinsohn continued to write, trying to show the Jews that they need not give up their own culture while sharing the culture of the world.

"Awake, My People"

Under Alexander II, the *Haskalah* movement gained many new followers. In 1863, in the city of St. Petersburg, a group of men organized a "Society for the Spread of Enlightenment Among the Jews of Russia." They wanted to make Russian, instead of Yiddish, the everyday language of the Jews. They wanted the Jews, who were usually tailors, cobblers, tradespeople, innkeepers, to turn more to farming and to the crafts. Like Levinsohn, they hoped that by introducing general subjects to the *Ḥeder* curriculum, they would open the doors of the Pale, letting in the light of a brighter world.

As the *Haskalah* movement spread, a new kind of literature developed. Using the Hebrew language, the *Maskilim* wrote articles, books and poems to rouse their people. "Awake, My People!" Judah Leib Gordon began one of his famous poems. See, his poem said, how the enslaved have been freed, and how the Jew is welcomed with a brotherly embrace.

In the ears of the *Yeshivah Baḥur*, bent over his Talmud by candlelight, the words of the Hebrew poets and

JUDAH LEIB GORDON

novelists rang like a distant bugle call. "Awake, My People!" How he yearned to rise from his bench and walk out of the crowded villages of the Pale, into green fields and sweet pine forests. Swaying endlessly over his Talmud, he dreamed of distant places, of white sails bending to green waters. Why were he and his people always cooped up, in the ghettos of Germany, in the Pale of Russia? What had they done? He closed his weary eyes and chanted the ancient words from the Talmud. "*Mai ka mash-ma lan*. . . . What do we learn from this?"

But the bugle call of the *Maskilim* sounded ever louder in the ears of the young people of the Pale. More books were written, more poems, more articles, to let light into the crowded Jewish villages. The holy language of the Bible had become the language of new thoughts and ideas, a language of stories and romance.

Sometimes, when the *Yeshivah Baḥur* was alone, he slipped a book from his pocket which he dared read only in secret. His heart beat fast as he opened Abraham Mapu's novel, *Ahavat Tziyon* (Love of Zion). It was a story of people who had lived long long ago, in the days of King Hezekiah. The candle burned lower and lower as he sat reading. The stars and the moon paled in the sky. But the *Bahur* did not notice. He sat on through the night, following the exciting adventures of young Tamar and Amnon, who loved each other, and who lived in sunny Judea, before the world had thought of ghettos and Pales to imprison them. Ah, thought the *Bahur*, as he closed his book at last, why could he too not live where sheep fed in green pastures? Why was life for him only a moving through narrow streets between home and *Yeshivah*, between *Yeshivah* and home?

Awakened by the *Haskalah*, many a *Bahur* finally rose from his Talmud, from the *mai ka mash-ma lan* he had repeated since childhood. Young Jewish men and women left the villages of the Pale and went to the Russian schools, hungry for the culture that was now theirs to enjoy. But many of them, in time, cut themselves off from their own people. Leaving the Pale, they left Jewish life as well. Aghast at the steady march of the younger *Maskilim* away from Judaism, Judah Leib Gordon wrote a poem in which he asked bitterly, "For Whom Do I Labor?"

Mendele Mokher Sefarim

Among the many writers who tried to brighten the dreary life in the Pale, one of the most famous was Shalom Jacob Abramovitch, who used the pen name *Mendele Mokher Sefarim*, Mendele the Bookseller. Mendele did not write

Enlightenment

only in Hebrew, but also in Yiddish, the language of the people, so that the uneducated as well as the educated could understand him. Nor did Mendele write of people distant in time or place. He wrote about the people about him, the people of the Pale. He wrote about beggars and innkeepers and respectable leaders of the *Kahal*. Though

MENDELE MOKHER SEFARIM

many of his works were critical of the Jews, beneath the criticism the readers felt his love for them, and his stories were read with delight in every village of the Pale.

Mendele was the first of a long line of famous writers who used Yiddish to create stories and novels. The despised language of the ghettos and the Pale became the language of a great literature which described the everyday life of the Jewish people.

"It Is Time to Go Home!"

There was one important reform, the most important of all, which many young Russian people wanted above everything—a constitution. A constitution meant political liberty, a representation of all the people in the government. But Czar Alexander feared to give his people a constitution. Too much freedom, he believed, would weaken the monarchy, or even lead to its overthrow.

As the demand for a democratic constitution grew more insistent, Alexander abandoned his program of reform. Russians petitioning for more rights for the people were sent to prison, or exiled to Siberia. But the enthusiastic university students, looking to France as their example, refused to give up their ideals of freedom. They organized into secret societies and met police terror with their own kind of terror, assassination.

On March 13, in 1881, on a street in St. Petersburg, Alexander II was assassinated when a dynamite bomb was hurled at him. The next day his son, Alexander III, came to the throne of Russia.

Enlightenment

"It is time to go home!" cried one of Alexander III's new advisers. By going home he meant returning to the oppression of the past, returning from the influence of the French ideals of liberty, to the brutality of the "Iron Czar."

Alexander too thought it was "time to go home." He knew of the poverty among his subjects. And he knew that discontent could swell into revolution which would wipe him and all Czars from the throne of Russia. But neither did he believe in giving the people the reforms they demanded. He decided to use an old trick which other tyrants had used before him. With his advisers, he planned to direct the attention of the discontented people away from their real oppressors, to a helpless minority, the Jews.

Rumors began to spread that the Jews were responsible for the assassination of Alexander II. There were Jews too among the revolutionists, as there were always Jews among fighters for freedom. But the number of the Jewish revolutionists was small. According to the rumors, however, the Jews were responsible not only for the death of Alexander, but for all the ills of Russia. Thus the way was paved for attacks against the Jews.

Pogroms

Six weeks after Alexander III came to the throne, the attacks began. No one talked of them openly, or mentioned how they started. But they were carefully organized, and it was suspected that they were directed by officers of the Czar. For they came in waves, and they always followed the same pattern.

The first attack, or pogrom, came in a town in the south of Russia. Mobs broke into Jewish homes and stores, spreading terror and ruin and death. For two days the mobs were permitted to do as they pleased, while the police stood by and watched. On the third day the pogrom was suddenly halted by the police.

From the south of Russia the pogroms spread northward. In each pogrom, the attackers, who were usually peasants, robbed and destroyed and killed for two days. And on the third day they were halted. They were stopped because the police did not want the rioters to get out of hand. They were to be used only to attack the Jews, and no more. So well had the rumors done their

SYNAGOGUE MURAL SHOWING VIEW OF JERUSALEM
(POLAND)

work, that many peasants were afraid not to attack the Jews, believing that they were following orders from the Czar.

The pogroms went on and on, while the civilized world watched in horror and protested to the Russian government. But most horrified and shocked by the pogroms were the *Maskilim*, the men who had tried to introduce the Jews to Russian and western culture. Thousands of Jews had responded to the call of the *Maskilim*, eager to be accepted by the Russians as brothers. But the government had met them not with the "brotherly embrace" Judah Leib Gordon had promised, but with pogroms.

The May Laws

The pogroms were not the last of the tragedies suffered by the Jews of Russia. In May, 1882, the May Laws were passed. These laws forced the Jews out of the small towns of the Pale into larger ones. The May Laws meant poverty or starvation for thousands of Jews, for the larger towns were crowded with tailors, innkeepers, tradesmen. Homeless and poverty-stricken, tens of thousands of Jews looked about them hopelessly, wondering where to go, or what to do.

East and West

Far across the ocean lay America, a land without kings or Czars or ghettos or Pales, a land where the oppressed from all parts of the world had found shelter. In the thousands, the Jews left Russia and sailed for America. Whole villages and towns of Jews uprooted themselves and streamed westward, to the friendly shores of the land of liberty. And a small trickle went east, to *Eretz Yisrael,* the Land of Israel. Like many Spanish exiles four hundred years back, they followed their hearts to the East.

For the Pupil

THINGS TO TALK ABOUT:

1. What is the meaning of the term, enlightenment?
2. What did the *Maskilim* hope to accomplish?
3. Why were the Jews of Russia used as a scapegoat?

THINGS TO DO:

1. Write the diary of a *Yeshivah Baḥur* leaving his native village and entering a Russian school. Was it difficult for him to leave home? Who were his new friends? What adjustments did he have to make?
2. Do some research on the life of the Jews in Russia. Try to get pictures of homes, *Ḥeders,* synagogues, costumes, villages, etc. Ask your librarian to help you find articles and books on the subject. When you have all your materials gathered, do a mural showing the life of the Russian Jews.

Teacher's Bibliography

Grayzel, Solomon, *A History of the Jews,* pp. 605-614.

Learsi, Rufus, *Israel,* pp. 462-477.

Margolis and Marx, *History of the Jewish People,* pp. 671-672; 686-687.

CHAPTER THREE

Auto-Emancipation

Without Messiah

Many changes took place in the Europe of the nineteenth century. Oppressed peoples threw off their oppressors and became nations. The Italian provinces united into a single kingdom. Rumania, Serbia, Bulgaria took their place in the family of nations. In the year 1870, the Germanic lands united into a single state, Germany.

Why not the Jews? some people asked.

For two thousand years they had been scattered over the face of the earth, suffering what no other people had ever suffered, slander, scorn, discrimination, poverty, crusades, *auto-da-fés,* expulsions, pogroms.

For two thousand years the Jews had kept alive the dream of returning to Zion, voicing it each year at the Passover *Seder:* "Next year in Jerusalem!" But only a handful of old men and women returned, year by year, to spend their last days in the Holy Land. With frenzy, the Jews had welcomed each false Messiah who came their way, promising peace, justice and nationhood. But each time their hopes had turned to ashes, and only their dreams remained.

Why must his people dream, while other people became nations? asked Moses Hess in Germany.

At about the same time, Zevi-Hirsch Kalischer, a rabbi in Berlin, was asking the same question. So were Peretz Smolenskin, in Vienna, and George Eliot, in England. Many people were asking themselves, why should not the Jews too become a nation?

Then the idea began to find its way into books.

"Looking Forward to a Land"

Moses Hess wrote a book, *Rome and Jerusalem,* in which he expressed the hope that Palestine would be colonized by the Jews, under the direction of a Jewish Congress. With the help of other nations, he believed that the Jews could once more become a nation.

In the same year, in 1862, Rabbi Kalischer produced a book in which he too appealed for the colonization of Palestine. His people must stop waiting for miracles, he said. They must learn to help themselves. The era of the Messiah, the days of peace and justice, would come only when the Jews were a nation on their own soil.

In Vienna, Peretz Smolenskin founded a magazine, *Ha-Shaḥar* (The Dawn). Smolenskin, who had traveled through Europe to observe the life of the Jews, appealed to them to stop abandoning their own religion in order to be like their neighbors. "You wish to be like other nations!" he cried. "So do I. . . . Find knowledge . . . do not be ashamed of the rock from which you are hewn . . . be hopeful, like all persecuted peoples . . . of the day when we too shall again inhabit the land which was and still is our own."

In England, George Eliot wrote a novel, *Daniel Deronda*. Through the words of her Jewish hero, George Eliot, although a Christian, spoke for the Jews.

> Looking forward to a land . . . our scattered people in all ends of the world may share the dignity of a national life. . . . Then our race (people) shall have a center, a heart and a brain; . . . the outraged Jew shall have a defense in the court of nations, as the outraged Englishman or American. And the world will gain as Israel gains. . . .

Words into Deeds

As the ideas found their way into words, so the words became deeds. Inspired by Rabbi Kalischer, Jewish university students in Vienna formed a society, *Kadimah*, which means both eastward and forward. Branches of *Kadimah* went up in other cities. In Russia and in other lands groups which called themselves *Ḥovevei Tziyon* (Lovers of Zion), were formed. In France, a society to protect Jews wherever protection was needed, had been founded in 1860. The society, which was called the *Alliance Israélite Universelle*, founded an agricultural school in Palestine, *Mikveh Israel*, Hope of Israel. The school stood alone, like a sentinel in the neglected land, waiting for colonists to come.

It did not have long to wait. The *Ḥovevei Tziyon* movement was growing, especially in Czarist Russia. Many young men and women had been awakened by the *Maskilim* to a love of their language, Hebrew, and to a love of their own culture. With this love came a desire to be a nation in the land that had once been theirs.

Auto-Emancipation

As many young people in Russia laid plans for returning to Zion, there arose a leader to encourage them. The leader was Leo Pinsker, a Jewish physician of Odessa. Pinsker had been one of the first of the *Maskilim*. He had hoped that the Jews would find emancipation through attending Russian schools. But the pogroms and the May Laws had destroyed his hopes. In 1882, twenty years after Moses Hess wrote his *Rome and Jerusalem*, Leo Pinsker wrote a pamphlet, *Auto-Emancipation*, which means, self-emancipation.

No one, said Pinsker, can emancipate the Jews, except the Jews. They had been walking the earth like a ghost for two thousand years, a dead nation. To become alive again, they must have their own land. They must learn to help themselves.

The pamphlet was read in every village of the Pale. Never had such words been spoken in Russia. There was to be no more dreaming of the Messiah, no more talk of

ISAIAH 2:5

Auto-Emancipation

miracles. The ghosts of two thousand years must straighten their backs and help themselves, said Pinsker.

"Come, Let Us Go Up"

Things began to happen more quickly now. The Societies of Ḥovevei Tziyon met in Germany and formed a federation, with Pinsker as its president. A new colony went up in Palestine, *Petaḥ Tikvah* (Gate of Hope). A group of young Russian Jews, mostly university students, came to Palestine to settle on the soil. Their slogan was BILU, the first letters of the Hebrew words, "House of Jacob, come, let us go up!" Hundreds of years back, the prophet Isaiah had spoken these words in Judea. Now came Isaiah's descendants to settle in the land of the prophets.

Others followed quickly, in small groups. They came to prepare a homeland for their people, and to blaze the trail for others who would follow.

They knew that the land had become poor and neglected. But in their minds they carried the descriptions they had read in the Bible—a land of milk and honey, of

בית יעקב

vineyards, fig trees, pomegranate and citron trees, a land of barley, wheat and rye.

They found none of these. What they found was the western wall of the Temple, which had become the Wailing Wall, where Jews came to weep and pray. They found poor families living on money which was sent them by Jews from all parts of the world. They found crooked tree stumps, miles of desertland, scrubby brush, swamps, malaria, trachoma, hostile Turkish officials.

But they set to work. They built barracks to live in. They drained swamps and slowly broke through the hard, stony soil. Many died, but others took their places. They worked feverishly, waiting for more settlers to come. From the west, help came. Baron Edmond de Rothschild, in Paris, sent seed, machinery, livestock. More permanent homes went up. More pioneers came, but always in small groups. Those who died of the diseases that ravaged the land were replaced by others. They came in tens, twenties, fifties, and they knew that they must have thousands.

At last a man called Theodor Herzl founded the movement which we know as Zionism. It was this movement which brought thousands into Palestine to turn the wasteland into a homeland.

THE TOMB OF RACHEL AT EFRATH, NEAR BETHLEHEM

᭡᭡ For the Pupil

THINGS TO TALK ABOUT:

1. Why did the idea of the Jews becoming a nation again become popular in the nineteenth century?
2. What did Smolenskin mean when he said, "Do not be ashamed of the rock from which you are hewn"? Compare this idea with that of Leopold Zunz, who believed that if the Jews knew themselves, they would regain the pride they had been deprived of during the Middle Ages.
3. "And the world will gain as Israel gains," said George Eliot, the English novelist. What did she mean by this statement?

THINGS TO DO:

Write to the Jewish National Fund for material on the rebuilding of Palestine. Tell them you would like stories and other materials, including pictorial, on the early and later pioneers. Start a scrapbook which will show the development of modern Israel from the founding of the first colony to the present time. Use pictures sent you by the J.N.F. Make your own pictures as well. Write stories based on the articles you read. Make a few maps to show where the new settlements went up. When you get to the sixth unit, you will find yourself doing more and more work on your scrapbook. Begin work on scrapbook now.

᭡᭡ Teacher's Bibliography

Grayzel, Solomon, *A History of the Jews,* pp. 664-670.
Learsi, Rufus, *Israel,* pp. 478-482.
Margolis and Marx, *History of the Jewish People,* pp. 679-680; 697-698.

CHAPTER FOUR

~~~ Zionism

A Correspondent in Paris

Until he saw them drown out the words of an innocent man with drums and heard the shouts of the mobs, Theodor Herzl had scarcely thought of himself as a Jew. He had been *Bar Mitzvah* when he was a boy in Budapest. And later, when he attended the University of Vienna, he had withdrawn from a fraternity because its leaders had made a ruling that no more Jews were to be admitted. But otherwise, there had been little to remind him that he was Jewish.

Why then, thought Theodor Herzl, should the trial of Alfred Dreyfus, a Jew, so disturb him? Dreyfus was a captain in the French army, and he had been accused of selling French military secrets to Germany. Whether Dreyfus was innocent Herzl did not know. But as they broke Dreyfus' sword and ripped the insignia from his uniform, the Jewish captain had cried through white lips, "I am innocent! Long live France!" Would a guilty man, wondered Herzl, have uttered this cry?

And why, he thought in agony, should the crowds watching the Jewish captain's degradation shout, "*A bas les Juifs!*" (Down with the Jews!) If one Jew was proved a traitor, should the crowds cry vengeance on all the Jews? And in France, cradle of liberty!

Theodor Herzl, Paris correspondent for the famous Vienna newspaper, *Neue Freie Presse,* slowly returned to his hotel, the cries of the mobs ringing in his ears. The tall, handsome man whose beauty was like that of a king of ancient days carved in stone, wrote a report of the trial of Alfred Dreyfus and dispatched it to his newspaper. But his heart and mind were filled with other things. Never before had it mattered to him that he was Jewish. He had always lived a carefree life, in Vienna, in Paris, traveling through Italy. He had moved in gay circles, on the boulevards and in the cafés. Now, at one stroke, the carefree life had ended. The man who had never heard of Hess, Smolenskin, Kalischer, Pinsker, the

DEGRADATION OF CAPTAIN DREYFUS, JANUARY 1895

Hovevei Tziyon, decided that his people must have a national home. He did not know that others had thought of it before him.

He tried to shake off the idea that he must do something about it. What could he, a journalist, do? He had no money, no followers. But wherever he went, whatever he did, the thought haunted him. He must do something to make a home for his people. And was it really so difficult to achieve? He would write out his ideas and present them to some famous Jewish leader who would then carry on the work. He would go to the rich Baron de Hirsch, who had tried to settle thousands of Jews in Argentina. Or he would go to the Rothschilds. There were many wealthy Jews. They would help.

Judenstaat

Then Theodor Herzl began to write the pamphlet that was to begin a new life for him. It was called *Judenstaat* (The Jewish State), and in it he expressed his great yearning for a homeland for his people. The only salvation for the Jews, he said, was a land of their own. Their emigration must take place in an orderly way, groups forming around their rabbis who would lead them to the Promised Land. First the poor would come, to develop the soil and the industries. They would work but seven hours a day, so that they would have leisure to enjoy the culture they would develop as a free people. The writers and artists and scholars would follow the workers. Then the rich would come. Theirs would be a model state, supported by all the powers of the world. On free soil, a nation of vigorous, creative men and women would arise. And as the Jews would create and grow strong, all the world would gain. Equal at last with all nations, the Jews would take their place in the family of nations.

"If you will it," said Herzl, "it is no legend."

Unfurling the Flag

Herzl had hoped that with the writing of *The Jewish State* his work would end. But he found that it had only begun. The pamphlet was published, and at once there was a storm of protest. He was attacked by those who believed in waiting for the Messiah. He was attacked by those who feared that the governments of the countries in which they lived would call them disloyal. To some, his ideas of a whole people returning to Zion seemed the dream of a madman.

But Herzl also received messages of encouragement from Russia, Hungary, Bulgaria. The messages were not from the rich and powerful, from whom he had expected the most help. They were from students, and from the humble among his people.

Overnight, Theodor Herzl found himself the leader of a movement, Zionism.

He interviewed kings and ministers of state, asking for their help. He went to see the Pope, and the ministers of Russia. He went to Turkey, to bargain with the sultan, ruler of Palestine, for a charter which would give the Jews the right to settle in Palestine. He gave himself no rest. Almost singlehandedly, he built up the movement of Zionism.

For gradually, as Herzl went from place to place, the movement grew. Thousands, then more thousands, joined behind the banner Herzl had unfurled. Only two years after Herzl had witnessed Dreyfus' degradation, he felt ready to call a Zionist Congress whose delegates, coming from every land, could speak in the name of their people to all the world.

In August, 1897, the delegates of the first Zionist Congress assembled in the little city of Basle, in Switzerland. To the delegates, and to the thousands of people who had sent them as their representatives, the congress seemed a wonderful thing. For hundreds of years they had been tucked away in ghettos and Pales. Now they came forth openly, to make plans, to discuss, while all the world listened.

Herzl entered the congress hall, stately as a prince in Israel. The delegates rose to their feet, cheering, shouting and weeping. For before them stood the man who had gathered them from every country and had given them dignity and pride. Tall, straight, regal in bearing, he reminded them of their kings of long ago, of David and Solomon who had ruled in splendor in the city of Jerusalem.

"If colonization is to continue at all," Herzl told the delegates, "it must continue on a large scale. A people can only help itself. If it cannot do this, then it cannot be helped...."

The Growth of Zionism

Many more thousands joined the Zionist movement.

HERZL ADDRESSING THE FIRST ZIONIST CONGRESS
AFTER A CONTEMPORARY DRAWING

From the land of pogroms and May Laws, Jews sent whatever they could spare to strengthen the movement. New congresses were held. The Jewish National Fund was set up to buy land for the Jewish people.

In the meantime, Herzl worked on. Though he had many aides to help him now, he still carried the leadership alone. He went to Palestine, where he saw the struggling colonies, waiting for help. He wrote a book, *Altneu-*

land (Old-New Land), in which he set forth his dream of what Palestine would some day be. He interviewed the kaiser of Germany, hoping that he would speak in his behalf to the sultan. He went to see the sultan again, who promised him a charter for Palestine if the Jews would pay his debts to the European countries. If he had had the money to give to the sultan at that moment, Herzl said later, he would have obtained the charter. But he did not have it, and he appealed to the rich again and again to help him. It was only the poor, however, who helped, with the few coins they could spare.

Herzl worked without pause or rest, till his heart gave out. In the year 1904, when he was forty-four years old, the founder of Zionism died. Herzl had given all that a man could give for his people, his life.

THEODOR HERZL

Returning to Zion

In the very year that Herzl died, new groups of settlers came to Palestine. This time they came not in groups of tens and twenties and fifties, but in the thousands. They still had no charter to settle in the land. Yet they came, most of them from Eastern Europe, where their suffering and poverty were greatest. For ten years the *Aliyah*, the "going up," continued, till the Jewish community in Palestine numbered one hundred thousand.

Life in Palestine was still difficult. The Turkish government was opposed to Jews buying land. There was still malaria, trachoma, yellow fever. The pioneers often had to fight off invaders while they put up barracks and water towers.

But slowly they won their battle. They founded colonies in wildernesses. Fields of wheat bloomed over land that had once been marshes. Trim farming settlements nestled in valleys, and under green hills. A stretch of sand dunes near Jaffa was transformed into a beautiful suburb named Tel-Aviv.

One of the People

Before Theodor Herzl had even dreamed his dream of Zionism, there lived a man in Russia who was teaching his people what it meant to love Zion. His name was Asher Ginzberg, but he did not use his name when he signed the articles he wrote. In his modesty, he called himself *Ahad Ha-Am*, One of the People.

In the most beautiful Hebrew that had been written

STREET IN TEL AVIV TODAY

in many centuries, *Ahad Ha-Am* wrote articles which challenged the aims of the Jews settling in Palestine. Love of Zion, said *Ahad Ha-Am,* must come before settlement in Palestine. Hebrew culture must be reborn even before the land was reborn. The people must strengthen their religion, their literature, their art. For only if they loved Judaism would they be able to survive the hardships of Palestine and build a rich and beautiful land. Numbers, said *Aḥad Ha-Am,* did not matter. One small colony, truly devoted to the ideals of their people, could accomplish more than many colonies which were interested only in escaping poverty and oppression.

In essay after essay, the scholar in Odessa brought his ideas before the people. And though many disagreed, and many felt that he was merely halting the movement toward emancipation, *Aḥad Ha-Am* continued to bring his criticism to the attention of his readers. Through the magazine he edited, *Ha-Shiloaḥ,* he influenced larger and larger numbers of Zionists.

As *Aḥad Ha-Am* had hoped, Hebrew culture blossomed in the blossoming land. The fighters of malaria, the drainers of swamps, the builders of cities and agricultural colonies, revived the ancient language of their ancestors. Gradually, Hebrew became the language of the land. Thus a new culture developed, stemming from the old culture. People and culture developed together in the old-new land.

∿∿ For the Pupil

THINGS TO READ:

1. Kalisch, Betty, *Watchmen of the Night,* "A Jewish State," page 198.
2. Levinger, Elma, *Great Jews Since Bible Times,* "The Story of a Dream That Came True," page 151.
3. Lurie, Rose, *The Great March,* Book Two, "If I Forget Thee," page 202.
4. Pessin, Deborah, *Giants on the Earth,* Part Two, "The Traitor," page 45, and "Without Messiah," page 52.
5. Pessin, Deborah, *Theodor Herzl,* Behrman House, New York, 1948.

THINGS TO TALK ABOUT:

1. What did Herzl mean when he said, "If you will it, it is no legend"?
2. Why did *Aḥad Ha-Am* believe that love of Zion should come before settlement of Zion?
3. Compare the academy of Yavneh, founded by Johanan ben Zakkai, with the Zionist Congress called by Herzl.

∿∿ Teacher's Bibliography

Bein, Alex, *Theodor Herzl,* Jewish Publication Society, 1940.

Grayzel, Solomon, *A History of the Jews,* pp. 671-684.

Herzl, Theodor, *The Jewish State,* Scopus Publishing Co., 1943.

Learsi, Rufus, *Israel,* pp. 515-526.

Margolis and Marx, *History of the Jewish People,* pp. 702-713.

Samuel, Maurice, *Harvest in the Desert,* Jewish Publication Society, 1944.

UNIT FIVE

In the Land of the Free

*GIVE me your tired, your poor,
Your huddled masses yearning to breathe free,
The wretched refuse of your teeming shore,
Send these, the homeless, tempest-tost to me.
I lift my lamp beside the golden door!*

> (From a sonnet by Emma Lazarus
> on the pedestal of the Statue of Liberty)

CHAPTER ONE

The First Settlers

To the New World

Soon after Columbus opened the route to America, a race began among the European powers to seize sections of the New World beyond the Atlantic Ocean. First in the race were Spain and Portugal. Then came Holland, England, France. Soldiers of these countries came to seize the land, and settlers came to settle upon it. Sometimes men and women came of their own accord, to escape the poverty and oppression of their native lands.

Jews came with the earliest settlers to find the freedom they had lost in the Old World. They came to the West Indies, and to the continent of South America. Later, when North America was opened for colonization, they came there too, to build a new life for themselves and their children.

In New Amsterdam

The first Jews who came as a group to North America were twenty-three settlers from Brazil. Brazil had first been occupied by the Portuguese, and the Jewish settlers had lived there as Marranos, observing their own customs in secret. But in 1630, when the Dutch captured Recife, the main city of Brazil, and other sections of the land from the Portuguese, the Jews were able to live openly as Jews. Then their community flourished, and many more Jews, most of them from Holland, joined the first Jewish settlers in Brazil. But the Portuguese recaptured Recife in 1654, and the Jews were given the choice of

The First Settlers

baptism or exile. Many Jews returned to friendly Holland, where they had enjoyed religious freedom. Twenty-three, however, found their way to the little Dutch settlement of New Amsterdam, on the eastern coast of North America. Here, they hoped, they would find the freedom their people enjoyed in Holland.

But the governor of New Amsterdam, Peter Stuyvesant, did not welcome the refugees from Brazil, as they had hoped he would. Peter Stuyvesant did not like Jews. He did not like Quakers either, or Lutherans, or Baptists. He liked no one, for that matter, whose religion was different from his. So Peter Stuyvesant told the Jews to find homes elsewhere. But the Jews refused to leave New Amsterdam. This was Dutch land, and they demanded the rights they had always enjoyed under the Dutch.

Peter Stuyvesant wrote to his employers in Holland, the Dutch West Indies Company, asking for permission to expel the newcomers from New Amsterdam. The Jews wrote letters too, to their friends in Holland, asking for help against Peter Stuyvesant. It happened that there were Jews among the investors in the Dutch West Indies Company. The company's directors also knew how bravely the Jews had fought in Brazil, giving their lives in the defense of Recife. When Peter Stuyvesant received his reply from the directors of the Dutch West Indies Company, he found, to his annoyance, that the Jews were to be permitted to remain in New Amsterdam.

But the contest between Peter Stuyvesant and the Jews was not over. The Jews might have the right to settle in New Amsterdam, but Peter Stuyvesant intended to

THE TIP OF MANHATTAN ISLAND, 1716-1718

give them no other right. All able-bodied Dutchmen in New Amsterdam, for example, were expected to do guard duty, for there was constant danger of Indian attacks. The Jews, Peter Stuyvesant decided, were to be excused from guard duty, but they were to be taxed instead. Led by Asser Levy, one of the boldest of the little band of refugees, the Jews fought for their right to stand guard, like all other able-bodied men of New Amsterdam. Peter Stuyvesant was forced, at last, to grant them this right, as he was forced to grant them other rights. There was one right, however, which the Jews did not win till the British conquered New Amsterdam and called it New York. This was the right to open a house of worship.

In the Harbor City

When the Jewish group of pioneers came to North America from Brazil, there were settlements besides New

The First Settlers

Amsterdam along the Atlantic seaboard. Some had been founded by men and women seeking religious freedom, and some by pioneers who had come to escape the poverty of the Old World. To the wilderness of Massachusetts the Pilgrims came, determined to worship God in their own way. But gaining freedom for themselves did not mean, to the Pilgrims, granting it to others. They permitted no one to settle in their colony who did not worship as they did.

There lived, among the Pilgrims, a minister whose name was Roger Williams. Roger Williams believed that all men should have freedom of conscience. His opinions did not please the Pilgrim elders, and in 1635, almost twenty years before the first group of Jews came to New Amsterdam, Roger Williams was banished from Massachusetts. In Rhode Island, which was then uncultivated territory, Roger Williams bought land from the Indians and founded a colony, which he called Providence. And because he granted religious freedom to all who came to settle there, a Jewish community, in time, developed in Newport, the harbor city of Rhode Island.

Most of the early Jewish settlers in America were merchants. They preferred, therefore, to live on the seacoast, in settlements where they could enjoy religious freedom. And so Jews who had once lived in Spain and Portugal came to Newport. Jews also came to Newport from Holland, from the West Indies, from South America. A few drifted in from the Germanic states, and from the distant lands of Eastern Europe.

The Jewish merchants traded with the Indians, buying their furs. They sent the furs and other American products to the West Indies and to the markets of Europe. When their vessels came streaming back into harbor, they carried cargoes of silk, laces, linen, books, needles, buckles, muslin. The merchants shipped their imported goods to the seacoast cities, and to the pioneers building settlements inland to the west.

Not all the Jews of Newport were traders, or merchant princes with fleets streaming back and forth across the ocean. There were carpenters, bakers, butchers, tinsmiths, among them. One Jewish settler introduced the preparation of whale oil for use in lamps. Another manufactured potash by a secret process. In whatever way they could, Jewish settlers helped the country grow.

Like almost every Jewish community that developed in America, the Jews of Newport built a synagogue. They wanted a place to worship, and a place where their children could learn the language, the religion, and the customs of their ancestors. And because many of them had been Marranos, or were descendants of Marranos, they built a secret exit in their synagogue, so strong in their minds were their memories of Spain and Portugal.

In their beautiful synagogue, which exists to this day, and which the government has set aside as a national shrine, Jews who had worshipped in secret in Spain and Portugal were at last able to worship openly. The Lopez, the Riveras, the Touros, the men and women with Spanish names whose ancestors had burned in the fires of the Inquisition, came to their synagogue dressed in silks and velvets and brocades. On freedom's soil, they lifted their voices proudly in the ancient prayers of their fathers.

SYNAGOGUE IN NEWPORT, R.I.

Celebration in Georgia

On a wide expanse of land which later developed into the city of Savannah, in the year 1733, a group of men and women were celebrating the new life that lay before them. Raising their mugs of beer, they drank to the health of James Oglethorpe, their kindly governor who had come with them from England. From the forests behind came the sweet smell of pine trees, and overhead the skies were clear and blue. Again and again the new colonists filled their mugs and drank. They drank to Oglethorpe, to freedom in America, to prosperity. Their voices rang loud and gay, re-echoing in the pine forests. They sported on the fresh, springy soil that had never been touched by the plow.

The men had been debtors in England. They had been flung into prison because they had been unable to pay their debts. James Oglethorpe, an Englishman, disliked the English system of imprisoning a man who could not pay his debts because of poverty. He laid before Parliament a plan for founding a colony in America with debtors from English prisons. Parliament advanced a sum of money for the project, a company was set up to direct

The First Settlers

the affairs of the colony, and Oglethorpe set out for America with his colonists.

So the colonists were celebrating, choosing the day when Oglethorpe was to apportion to each of them a plot of land. They were celebrating because of the new homes they would build, and because of the dark, rich earth which they would plow and sow, and whose crops they would harvest.

The New Arrivals

Suddenly, as though by a signal, the merrymaking stopped. For coming toward them along the path from the sea, the colonists saw a group of men and women and children whom they did not know. The manner of the strangers was hesitant, as though they were uncertain of the welcome they would receive.

In the heavy silence about them, the newcomers explained that they were Jews. Most of them had fled from Spain to England, and from England they had sailed for America. Their ships, tossed about by storms, had brought them to North Carolina. But they had remained in North Carolina for only a short time before sailing for the new colony of Georgia.

A murmur went up among the English colonists. They did not want Jews among them, they said. But James Oglethorpe, the kindly governor who hated persecution, made the forty newcomers welcome. Then he wrote to the trustees of the company in England, informing them of the arrival of the Jews.

The trustees were as prejudiced as the colonists. They wrote to the governor, telling him to keep the Jews from settling in Georgia. Oglethorpe, however, decided to do as he pleased. Again he wrote to the trustees, praising the thrift and industry of the Jewish settlers, and telling them about Dr. Samuel Nunez, who was caring for the health of the colonists. Since Governor Oglethorpe was not permitted to give the Jewish settlers land, he sold them land. And in time, their differences forgotten, Jews and Christians felled trees and cleared forests and built homes together.

Growing with America

So it was in many early colonies in America. Where the Jews were given freedom of religion, they came, settled, and helped America grow. Even before the founding of Savannah, William Penn had founded a colony in Pennsylvania, offering religious freedom to all who came to settle there. And many Jews came, finding their way to Lancaster, Easton, Philadelphia. They built stockades and log cabins. They traded with the Indians. They helped push back the wilderness. They sent barges of goods up and down the rivers. Jews also came to the colony of Charleston, in South Carolina, for John Locke, the English philosopher, had drawn up a constitution for South Carolina which gave its settlers religious freedom.

The freedom the Jews enjoyed was not always complete freedom. A Jew might be given the right to worship as he pleased, but not the right to vote, or to hold office. For many Christian settlers came to the New World with the prejudices of the Old World. Step by step, however, as America grew, the ideal of freedom also grew.

God's American Israel

The Bible was a familiar book in many American homes. It lay on the mantelpiece over the hearth, to be read whenever there was time. Men read it by firelight, after their work in the field. They read it in times of stress, and in times of joy. They knew the stories of Moses leading the Israelites away from the slavery of Egypt, and the words of the prophets demanding justice. The Bible was as familiar to the American as the air he breathed.

On the eve of the American Revolution, in churches all over the land, pastors delivered sermons based on the ideals of justice and freedom found in the Bible. They spoke of King George as a Pharaoh, and of the Americans as enslaved Israelites. The new nation of Americans, said

Dr. Ezra Stiles, president of Yale College, was God's American Israel, and George Washington was an American Joshua, leading his people to liberty.

When Congress decided to draw up a seal for the new American government, it called upon Jefferson, Franklin and Adams to submit an idea for the seal. The idea submitted was not accepted by Congress, but it revealed the love of the Founding Fathers for the Bible. Jefferson, Franklin and Adams suggested, as a seal for the American government, a picture of Pharaoh pursuing the Israelites as they crossed the Red Sea. And around the picture they suggested the words: "Rebellion against tyrants is obedience to God."

On the Liberty Bell in Philadelphia were engraved the famous words from the Bible: "Proclaim liberty throughout the land unto all the inhabitants thereof." The ideals of justice developed in ancient Israel had found root in the fresh soil of America.

Rebellion Against Tyrants

The Jews gave more than the ideals of their Bible to the American Revolution. Though there were some Tories among them, as there were among all American groups, most of the Jews stood behind the young government struggling for independence. They fought wherever there was fighting to be done. They were with George Washington in Valley Forge. They fought in the front lines and behind the lines. Jewish merchants signed the Non-Importations Resolutions, which boycotted goods from England. Jewish ship owners converted their vessels to privateers, so that they could prey on English ships. Isaac Moses and Co. sent their sloops, Chance and Fox, to destroy English ships and seize their cargoes. Other Jews, too, together with Christian merchants, used their converted vessels to wage war with the British on the high seas.

Haym Salomon

When the British took New York, during the American Revolution, they arrested a frail young man whose name was Haym Salomon. Haym Salomon had come from Poland, a land where his people were oppressed, to find freedom in America. In New York, he had joined the Sons of Liberty, an underground movement of American patriots.

It happened that Haym Salomon knew several languages, German, Polish, Russian. When this became known to the prison officials, they decided to make use of him. There were many Hessians among the British soldiers, men whom King George had hired from the Prince of Hesse to fight in his armies. Hesse was a German province, and the Hessians naturally spoke German. It was decided that Haym Salomon was to act as interpreter for a Hessian general.

Because of his position, Salomon was now given greater liberty. But he used his liberty to help American prisoners escape, and to persuade Hessian soldiers to desert to the Americans. Again Salomon was arrested, but this time he managed to escape. He fled to Philadelphia, and a short time later he was joined there by his wife and child.

Haym Salomon was a business man. In a little shop on Front Street, he went on with his business, which the British had interrupted when they entered New York. Most of the money he made he lent to the government, to buy food, clothing, munitions for the soldiers. When the government could not pay members of Congress, they often came to the little broker on Front Street, for they knew he would never refuse help.

Haym Salomon gave all he had for the revolution. Coming from the Old World of oppression, he gave whatever he could to make America free.

Proclaim Liberty

The war with the Redcoats was over at last. In Philadelphia, the Liberty Bell pealed out its message of

ROBERT MORRIS · GEORGE WASHINGTON · HAYM SALOMON

freedom: "Proclaim liberty throughout the land unto all the inhabitants thereof."

For the countries of Europe, where kings still ruled by "divine right" and peasants toiled in the fields of the noblemen, America became the model of a free republic. The Declaration of Independence stated that all men were created equal. The Bill of Rights granted religious liberty to all. To every man and woman, regardless of race or religion, were given the rights to life, liberty and the pursuit of happiness.

Now the states began to draw up their constitutions. Some states granted the Jews full rights, as did the Federal constitution. Some granted them only religious freedom. In some states, the struggle for civil rights went on for years, with Christians and Jews fighting together for the Jewish inhabitants of the states. But at last the Jews won complete freedom in every state of the land. The opportunities of America, the land they had helped to build, opened wider than ever before them.

For the Pupil

THINGS TO READ:

1. Leonard, Oscar, *Americans All,* "He fought for His Rights," page 25, "The Merchant Prince," page 29, "And Some Helped Washington," page 35.
2. Levinger, Elma, *Great Jews Since Bible Times,* "The Man Who Gave Everything," page 122, "Judah Touro," page 130.
3. Pessin, Deborah, *Giants on the Earth,* Part Two, "Son of Liberty," page 76, "Judah Touro Spends a Day," page 95.

THINGS TO TALK ABOUT:

1. How do you explain the fact that some people, in search of religious freedom in America, refused to give it to others?
2. In what way did the Bible influence the thinking of the Founding Fathers of America?

THINGS TO DO:

1. Dramatize the story of the coming of the Jews to Georgia.
2. If you live somewhere near Newport, try to arrange a trip to see the famous synagogue of that city.

Teacher's Bibliography

Friedman, Lee M., *Jewish Pioneers and Patriots,* Jewish Publication Society, 1942.

Grayzel, Solomon, *A History of the Jews,* pp. 549-563.

Goodman, Abram V., *American Overture: Jewish Rights in Colonial Times,* Jewish Publication Society, 1947.

Learsi, Rufus, *Israel,* pp. 393-401.

Lebeson, Anita, *Jewish Pioneers in America,* Behrman's Book House, 1938.

CHAPTER TWO

New Builders of America

After Waterloo

When Napoleon was defeated at Waterloo in 1815, liberty for the Jews was defeated in the countries he had conquered. In the Germanic lands, the rulers tried to wipe out the reforms Napoleon's armies had brought with them. Peasants and city workers lost the few rights they had won. Some Germans, bitter at having been defeated by the French, began to talk of themselves as being superior to the French, and to other nations. They talked of the Jews, who had been in the Germanic lands before them, as strangers. Again the Jews found themselves back in the ghettos, attacked, deprived of their rights, taxed into poverty.

But now the Jews, having tasted liberty, were not content to suffer in silence. They had heard of America, which had boldly proclaimed that all men were created equal. Other people had found freedom across the sea. Why could they too not leave their ghettos, they asked, and find the freedom others had found?

It was the poor and uneducated Jews who came to America in the years following 1815. The richer Jews, and those who had attended the universities, still hoped to find happiness in their native lands. But thousands of the poor left the ghettos. Singly, in families, in groups, they sailed for America.

In the New World

Everything seemed strange and new to the immigrants on American soil—the language, the clothes, the manners, the customs of the people. There were no ghettos, no fingers pointing at them because they were Jews, no ridicule or scorn. And strangest of all, every man stood equal before the law of America.

The German Jewish immigrant looked about him. He found that America was a large and plentiful land. Along the eastern coast busy industrial cities had developed. Farther west lay smaller cities and towns and farmland. And still farther west stretched the Mississippi Valley, into which pioneers were making their way. Beyond the Mississippi Valley lay great rolling prairies, green plains and craggy mountains, virgin forestland, winding rivers. On and on America stretched, with room for millions of immigrants to build her cities and farms.

The Jewish Peddler

The German Jewish immigrants of the early nineteenth century knew little about tilling the soil, for in their native lands they had been driven from the soil. Some, therefore, remained in New York City. Some went to Philadelphia, or to other industrial cities. And some became peddlers.

With the little money he had, the peddler bought trinkets, needles, thread, pots, pans, rolls of calico, ribbons, lace. And with his pack of merchandise on his back, he made his way westward. In the settlements beyond the coastal cities, the peddler went from house to house, selling his wares. When his pack was empty he bought more goods. Often he made his way farther west, into the Mississippi Valley. And often he went beyond it, following the trail of the pioneers. Hundreds and hundreds of miles inland he went, into Ohio, Illinois, Kansas, Nevada, over prairies and waterways and through mountain passes. The former dweller of the dark, narrow ghetto now had land without measure about him, and the open sky over his head.

The Jewish peddler was joyfully hailed as he came over the lonesome roads to the isolated homesteads. Families ran out to meet him, offering him rest and a place to sleep. For the peddler brought to the pioneers a glimpse of the civilized world back east. He told them news of the cities and of the settlements through which he had traveled. He held them entranced with tales of his boyhood days across the sea. His pack was a treasure chest, with its shining copper pots, with cloth for dresses and curtains, bags of tobacco for the men, and sometimes toys for the children.

With his savings, the peddler often bought a horse and wagon to make his work easier. Then he sent for his family in the old country to join him. Sometimes, when he came to a settlement where he felt he would like to live, he set up a store in a log cabin, or in a shack. From the neighboring farms came the homesteaders, to buy their grain, coffee, sugar, coils of rope, nails, tobacco, cloth, needles, occasional delicacies brought from the cities in the east.

Time went by and new settlers came. The small settlement gradually grew into a town. Lanes were paved and became streets. New houses went up. The peddler, with his little store on Main Street, became busier than ever.

He needed more room, more goods, more help than his family could give him. He moved into larger quarters. He bought larger supplies of merchandise. He hired people to help him. And still the town grew, and with it the store of the Jewish peddler.

Many towns became large cities, and many a small store became a large department store. And many a peddler who had started out as a poor, bewildered immigrant, became a rich member of his community.

Building Communities

When a man made good in the new country, the news reached his friends in the old country. Then they too crossed the ocean, eager for the free life of America. The newcomers often made their way to the towns and settlements of the earlier immigrants, for they felt more comfortable with people they knew and understood. The earlier settlers helped the later ones find work and a place to live. They helped them learn the language and the customs of the land.

As soon as they were able, the small groups of German Jewish settlers would open a synagogue, so that they could worship together. The synagogue was Orthodox, as it had been in their native land. Often they formed lodges, where they could get together for friendship sake, or to discuss matters which interested them all. The lodges were also mutual aid societies. They had loan funds, to help one another till they found work, or when they were sick, or to help other newcomers from their home towns. In this way Bnai Brith was founded in New York City in 1843 by twelve Jewish immigrants who called themselves Bundes Brüder. In time Bundes Brüder became Bnai Brith, which grew and grew, till today it has thousands of members, with branches all over the country.

New Arrivals

In 1848, all of Europe rumbled with revolution. Nations wanted to be free of foreign rule. In some countries, the people wanted to be free of their own oppressors.

In the Germanic lands, Jews and Christians fought side by side to end tyranny and to bring liberty to the people. But the revolutionary uprisings were so cruelly crushed, that thousands of men and women fled to America to escape the fury of the rulers they had tried to overthrow.

For about thirty years they kept coming. Thousands upon thousands of Christians and Jews left the Germanic lands and came to America. At the time of the Civil War, the Jewish community of America numbered about 150,000.

The new Jewish settlers spread over America, often joining those who had come before them. Many of the Jews coming from the Germanic lands had lived in the larger cities. Some had attended the universities and were familiar with the culture of western Europe. They had attended Reform temples, preferring them to the Orthodox synagogues of the ghettos. When they came to America, they brought with them the ideas of Reform Judaism. Instead of Orthodox synagogues, which the earlier Jewish settlers from Germany had built, many of the new arrivals built Reform temples, or attended those which had already been established before their coming.

Civil War

As America developed, the north grew more and more industrial, while the south developed its plantation system. But there came a time when North and South opposed each other on the question of slavery. In the South, where plantation owners used thousands of slaves to raise their cotton and tobacco, the people took slavery for granted, and naturally opposed all efforts to abolish it. In the industrial North, however, where men received wages for the work they did, slavery was condemned. Many Americans, remembering the oppression they themselves had suffered, wanted no form of tyranny in the New World.

Like the rest of the population, the Jews too were

divided. Some of the very earliest of the Jewish settlers had plantations in the South, and the greater number of them, like their Christian neighbors, favored slavery. But the hundreds of thousands who had fled from the Germanic lands were opposed to slavery.

There were Jews with John Brown in his fight against slavery. Jews were among the Republican delegates who nominated Abraham Lincoln for the presidency of the United States. Dr. David Einhorn, a rabbi in the pro-slavery city of Baltimore, had to flee for his life because he had preached against slavery.

When the Civil War broke out, however, the issue was not slavery, but union. Abraham Lincoln, president of the United States, wanted to keep the slave states from seceding and setting up a government of their own. But as the war dragged on, the question of slavery became more and more important.

The Jews fought on both sides in the Civil War, with the majority in the Union armies. With the rest of America, they fought the fight which was to decide the future of the country, whether it was to be slave or free. And the decision of America was freedom.

For the Pupil

THINGS TO READ:

1. Leonard, Oscar, *Americans All,* "He Scored a Point," page 79, "Kind as a Father," page 95, "He Captured a Dictator," page 101, "The Fighting Doctor," page 107, "They Were Friends of Lincoln," page 114, "The Brains of the Confederacy," page 123.

New Builders of America

2. Lurie, Rose, *The Great March*, "Who Will Build Ararat," page 150, "Of Thee I Sing," page 179.
3. Pessin, Deborah, *Giants on the Earth*, Part One, "Noah's Ark," page 89, Part Two, "Emma Lazarus Comes Home Again," page 9.

THINGS TO TALK ABOUT:

1. Why did the defeat of Napoleon mean an end of freedom for the Jews in the Germanic lands?
2. What difficulties did the German Jewish immigrant have to overcome when he came to America?

THINGS TO DO:

1. Write the adventures of a German Jewish peddler. Make some illustrations for your story.
2. If there is a branch of the Bnai Brith in your city, invite one of its members to come to your class to tell you about Bnai Brith, how it started, how it grew, what it does.
3. Read some of the Negro Spirituals. Show how the ideas in many of them come from the Bible.

Teacher's Bibliography

Eisenberg, Azriel, *Modern Jewish Life in Literature*, "The New World," pp. 67-103.

Finkelstein, Louis, editor, *The Jews*, Volume I, Jewish Publication Society, 1949, Anita Lebeson's article, "The American Jewish Chronicle," pp. 313-347.

Grayzel, Solomon, *A History of the Jews*, pp. 615-628.

Learsi, Rufus, *Israel*, pp. 482-492.

CHAPTER THREE

Builders of Judaism

A Rabbi in Bohemia

One day, a young rabbi in Bohemia, Isaac Mayer Wise, came upon a set of American English prints in a little book store in the city of Prague. Among the prints he found some old newspapers containing the debates that had taken place on the American Constitution. As the young rabbi studied the prints and the journals, the world in which he lived seemed to fade away into the past. Only America seemed real. Isaac Mayer Wise determined to come to America. With his wife and young child, he left Bohemia, and in 1846, from the deck of the ship bringing him to a new life, he caught his first glimpse of New York.

Teaching Reform Judaism

Rabbi Isaac Mayer Wise, who believed in Reform Judaism, found that the movement was still weak in America. The majority of the Jews, even those from the Germanic lands, preferred Orthodox Judaism. They wanted their prayers in Hebrew, rather than in English or in German. They preferred to keep, in their prayers, the idea of the Messiah and the hope of a return to Zion. Nor did they

Builders of Judaism

want to give up any of the laws of the Talmud, or the customs they had inherited from the past. Rabbi Wise determined to spread the ideals he believed in, and to strengthen Reform Judaism in America.

Isaac Mayer Wise began in Albany, where he became the rabbi of an Orthodox congregation. But so opposed were many members of the congregation to changes in their services, however slight, that he was finally forced to resign. The members of the congregation whom he had won to his side, however, set up a Reform congregation, and Rabbi Wise became its leader.

Free now to work as he wished, Rabbi Wise introduced some of the ideas of Reform Judaism into his temple. But what made Rabbi Wise's name known to the Jews of America were the articles he wrote. Rabbi Wise saw many of the younger generation of Jews, those who had been born in America, abandoning the Jewish faith. They had never studied the literature of their people, as their fathers had. And scattered over America, there was noth-

ISAAC MAYER WISE

ing to unite them. Rabbi Wise also knew that there were hundreds of congregations in America, each with its own synagogue, each synagogue with its own rules and regulations. In addition, there was no school for training American rabbis. Many German immigrants had gone from poverty to comfort, and even to wealth. Still they looked to Europe for their rabbis.

In his articles, Rabbi Wise called for the unity of all the American Jewish congregations. He believed that the American Jews must train their own rabbis, instead of bringing them from the countries of Europe. If all the scattered congregations united, Rabbi Wise believed, they would be able to establish a school for the training of American rabbis.

Besides working for unity, Rabbi Wise also spread the ideals of Reform. Judaism, he said, must be adjusted to the free spirit of America. Only by abandoning the old practices which had become meaningless, could this be done. "Judaism," said Rabbi Wise, "has become a set of unmeaning practices. . . . Therefore we demand reforms. All unmeaning forms must be laid aside as outworn garments. . . . The internal spirit of Judaism must be expounded (explained). . . . We must inform our friends and opponents that there is a Judaism independent of its forms, and that this is Judaism emphatically. . . ."

Building a Center

In 1854, Rabbi Wise was called to Cincinnati to lead the congregation known as Bene Yeshurun. Cincinnati had long been a center for German Jews. With the coming of Rabbi Wise, it also became a center for Reform Judaism.

For the remainder of his life, Rabbi Wise lived in Cincinnati, leading his congregation, writing, organizing, teaching. He wrote a new prayerbook, *Minhag America*, which was used by his own congregation and which he hoped would in time become the prayerbook for all American Jews. He founded an English newspaper, the *Israelite*, and for those who could read only German, he founded a German one, the *Deborah*. Through his two publications, Rabbi Wise was able to reach many readers, bringing before them the ideas of Reform Judaism.

THE HEBREW UNION COLLEGE IN CINCINNATI

In time, the work of Rabbi Wise began to bear fruit. In the year 1873, delegates of thirty-four congregations gathered in Cincinnati and established the Union of American Hebrew Congregations. Two years later, in the same city, the Hebrew Union College was founded to train American-born rabbis. Finally, Rabbi Wise organized the Central Conference of American Rabbis, which was to meet, each year, to discuss the problems and aims of Reform Judaism.

The work begun by Rabbi Wise did not end with his death. Year by year, Reform congregations continued to join the Union of American Hebrew Congregations. And year by year, young American rabbis were graduated from the Hebrew Union College to take their places on the pulpits of America's Reform temples.

Historical Judaism in America

Many Jewish leaders and rabbis had hoped that the Union of American Hebrew Congregations would serve all the Jews of America. They had hoped that it would be a union of all the Jewish congregations. But not long after it was founded it became apparent that it could not serve all the Jews of the country. There were many Jewish leaders who agreed that Jewish life in America called for some form of adjustment to the conditions and spirit of the New World. But Reform Judaism, they felt, had gone too far in its break with the past. They, too, felt that Judaism was not static and unchanging, but a living organism which must necessarily develop with the times. But, they said, they did not believe in eliminating the basic ideals in their way of life—Hebrew as the language of prayer, the dietary laws, the idea of the Messiah. Change, they believed, must take place, but without breaking the continuity of Jewish life.

In 1887 a group of Jewish leaders and rabbis who believed in Conservative Judaism opened a school for American rabbis in New York City, the Jewish Theological Seminary of America. Sabato Morais, a rabbi of Philadelphia who had supported but later had withdrawn from the Union of American Hebrew Congregations, became the Seminary's first president. It was not, however, till the coming of Solomon Schechter, in 1902, that the Jewish Theological Seminary became a key in-

THE JEWISH THEOLOGICAL SEMINARY OF AMERICA IN NEW YORK

stitution in American life and the center for the movement of Conservative Judaism.

A Scholar in Cambridge

Solomon Schechter taught at Cambridge University. But although he taught at Cambridge, he was not a native of England. Solomon Schechter was born in a small town in Rumania, where he lived till he was a young man. The early years of Schechter's life were spent in studying Hebrew literature. When he left Rumania for Vienna, however, he also devoted himself to the literature and science of the world about him. His fame as a scholar soon spread, and he was invited to teach at Cambridge University.

One day, as Schechter was sitting in his study at Cambridge, two English women came to see him. They had been touring Palestine, they told him, and there they had bought some scraps of old parchment upon which was writing they could not understand. They knew that Solomon Schechter was a scholar. Would he like to see the parchment and see what he could make of it?

Solomon Schechter took the faded parchment scraps and looked at them. He took his magnifying glass and looked at them again. He put down all but one scrap, which he studied closely. And suddenly the glass began to tremble in his hand and he wanted to cry out for joy. For Solomon Schechter was holding a treasure. It was a bit of parchment from an ancient Hebrew manuscript, many hundreds of years old. *Ecclesiasticus,* it was called, or the Book of Ben Sirah, and it was a book of wise sayings by a man called Ben Sirah. The world had only the Greek translation of the Book of Ben Sirah. Scholars had been seeking the Hebrew book for many, many years. And here, in his hand, Solomon Schechter was holding a scrap of the original Hebrew manuscript. But where was the rest of the Ben Sirah manuscript?

The Discovery

For many days, Solomon Schechter pondered the question. He knew that Jews never destroyed their books. When books became too old for use, they buried them, as though they had once had life. Most synagogues had a special room for putting away old books and manuscripts. A *Genizah*, such a room was called, for *Genizah* means hidden. Where, in the neighborhood of Palestine,

Schechter wondered, could there be an ancient *Genizah* which had withstood the ravages of time? Surely it must be in Egypt, the land where the intense heat was so dry, that it acted as a preservative against decay. Only in Egypt could a *Genizah* containing the Ben Sirah manuscript have survived.

Solomon Schechter went to Egypt, to the city of Cairo, and on to the ancient synagogue called the Synagogue of Ezra the Scribe. He found the *Genizah* at the end of a long gallery. The *Genizah* had neither windows nor doors. A hole in the wall, reached by a ladder, was its only opening.

After receiving permission from the rabbi to take whatever he liked from the *Genizah,* Solomon Schechter climbed the ladder and let himself down into the chamber of old Hebrew books.

The room was dark and thick with dust. The slightest stirring of the foot, the least movement of the body, raised a cloud of dust. Everywhere, old books and manuscripts lay in heaps, some already crumbled to dust, some falling apart at the touch of the hand.

Solomon Schechter moved about cautiously. Yet the dust rose in a thick cloud, forcing its way into his mouth and nostrils, settling on his lungs. For days he worked in the dark chamber among the heaps of parchment and papyrus scrolls and books as ancient as the synagogue itself. And at last, among the dusty heaps of old manuscripts, he found the Hebrew Ben Sirah.

Ben Sirah was not the only important book or manuscript Solomon Schechter found, but it was the most famous. When his work in the *Genizah* was finished, Solomon Schechter sent his papers and books and manuscripts to Cambridge in crates. Then he returned to England, where he spent many years sorting and studying the treasure he had found in Cairo.

The scholar who had found the Ben Sirah manuscript became more famous than ever. In 1902, after the death of Sabato Morais, Dr. Schechter was invited to come to America, to become the president of the Jewish Theological Seminary. Dr. Schechter, in turn, invited a number of young, distinguished scholars to serve on the faculty of the Seminary. It was then that the Seminary gained in reputation and scholarship. So great was the influence of its president on the Seminary, that people often called it the Schechter Seminary.

Builder of Historical Judaism

Dr. Schechter, who became an important leader of the Conservative movement, also believed that the Jews must make adjustments in their customs to life in America, while at the same time preserving the ideals and traditions that had persisted through the ages. "Judaism is a positive religion," said Dr. Schechter, "with a Sacred Writ and a continuous tradition. . . . It has distinct precepts, and usages, and customs, consecrated by . . . Israel through thousands of years, and hallowed by the agony and the tears of the martyrs."

Dr. Schechter realized that in Judaism, as in most

important matters, there must be difference of opinion. Despite these differences, however, he believed that there must be unity among all the Jews scattered throughout the world. Not only, said Dr. Schechter, must there be world unity, but also unity with the generations of Jews past, and with the generations of Jews to come. Dr. Schechter saw Judaism as an unbroken chain, reaching from the far past through the present and into the future.

But unity with the past meant knowledge of the past, for a man could not continue what he did not understand. Dr. Schechter therefore tried to bring to the Seminary a respect and love for scholarship, so that Judaism might better be understood by the Seminary's students, and eventually by the Jews of the country.

In 1913, Dr. Schechter founded the United Synagogue of America, which was an organization of Conservative congregations. And some years later, the graduates of the Jewish Theological Seminary and other Conservative rabbis founded the Rabbinical Assembly of America, where they could discuss the problems of Conservative, or Historical Judaism.

The Teachers Institute

In order to bring Jewish culture to the Jewish children, Dr. Schechter established the Teachers Institute of the Jewish Theological Seminary, a school for the training of teachers. He appointed Dr. Mordecai M. Kaplan, a graduate of the Jewish Theological Seminary, dean of the Institute. Under Dr. Kaplan's leadership, American-of a large and modern building was laid in the upper section of New York City. Yeshivah then became Yeshivah College. Here students could train for becoming Orthodox rabbis, or for other professions. Finally, in 1945, Yeshivah College became Yeshivah University. Thus Yeshivah developed gradually from its humble beginnings on the lower East Side to a university, serving Jewish needs in both religious and secular fields.

Growing Up

Conservative and Reform and Orthodox Judaism all grew strong in the land which gave them freedom to grow. All three groups made plans for the future. All stood ready to welcome new immigrants to America, and to share with them what they had built.

ᨆᨆ For the Pupil

THINGS TO READ:

1. Kalischer, Betty, *Watchmen of the Night,* "In the Promised Land," page 187.
2. Levinger, Elma, *Great Jews Since Bible Times,* "An American Rabbi," page 147, "The Scholar Who Found Hidden Treasure," page 152.
3. Lurie, Rose, *The Great March,* Book Two, "The Hidden Treasure," page 217.
4. Pessin, Deborah, *Giants on the Earth,* "I took a Daring Leap," page 79, "Rescued," page 89.

THINGS TO TALK ABOUT:

1. Why was it possible for Reform, Conservative and Orthodox Judaism to develop side by side in America?
2. The American coins have inscribed upon them the words: "*E Pluribus Unum*" (Out of Many, One). This means that America is made up of many different peoples. Discuss this conception.

THINGS TO DO:

Visit a Conservative, an Orthodox, a Reform synagogue during services. What differences do you notice in their way of worship?

ᴡᴡᴡ Teacher's Bibliography

Finkelstein, Louis, *The Jews*, Volume One, "Jewish Religious Life and Institutions in America," by Moshe Davis, pp. 354-443.

Ginzburg, Louis, *Students, Scholars and Saints*, "Solomon Schechter," pp. 241-251.

Grayzel, Solomon, *A History of the Jews*, pp. 629-631; 696-700.

CHAPTER FOUR

Settlers From Eastern Europe

In the Pale

During the last quarter of the nineteenth century, life became unbearable for the Jews in the Pale of Settlement. Crowded together in their little towns, the Jewish tailors, cobblers, blacksmiths, storekeepers, carpenters, could barely earn enough to keep their families from starving. Outside the Pale stretched a giant country called Russia. Russia was where the mighty Czar lived, the Czar who was their oppressor. Russia had policemen and soldiers whom they feared. Russia had millions of ignorant, poverty-stricken peasants who believed that the Jews were responsible for their misery, for so they had been told. Russia was vast and brutal and filled with terror.

The Jews, huddled together in the crowded towns of the Pale, drew what happiness they could from the study of their Torah, from the Sabbath and their beautiful festivals bringing memories of their people's past. Now and then they heard of pogroms, of mobs breaking into Jewish towns to loot and kill. And in each town where the news reached the Jews prayed for the dead victims and for themselves, hoping that they would somehow manage to escape the pogroms.

And suddenly, down the narrow, dirt lanes of a town,

a group of frightened Jews would come, clutching a few possessions to their breasts—a few feather pillows, some articles of clothing, books, a precious family heirloom. The Jewish cobblers and tailors and blacksmiths and storekeepers would come running from their little wooden houses and surround the frightened refugees, waiting to hear their story.

And the story was always the same. The refugees were either fleeing from a pogrom, which they knew had been secretly organized by the government, or they had been driven from their town by the Czar's police.

Everyone tried to help the homeless victims. Samuel, the carpenter, who never had enough work, invited one family to sleep in his kitchen, crowding his crowded family even more. Dinah the widow had a room to spare. Sender, who drove a wagon for a living, said he had room on his tile stove for several children. Nathan, the mender of pots and kettles, said he could manage to squeeze a few guests into his parlor. Some could sleep in the synagogue, some in Tobiah's inn, on the wooden benches.

Gradually, the refugees found themselves homes of their own. If there were two tailors in town, there were now three, although there had not been work enough for the two. Cobblers without shoes to mend sat in their little shops wondering whether some other occupation might not have been better after all, and wondering where they would get money to buy food for the Sabbath.

As things were settling down again, news came of other pogroms, or of new raids on nearby towns, forcing the Jews into smaller towns. And sometimes a crowd of drunken peasants came streaming into the dingy streets, shouting and cursing. A pogrom had finally overtaken a town that had thus far remained untouched. The peasants in the neighborhood had been stirred up by government agents to attack the Jews. Living in hovels, taxed till they had barely enough to keep alive, the peasants had always lived a life of misery. When they were told that the Jews were to blame for their suffering, they came to avenge themselves, armed with clubs and knives and pitchforks.

To America

Finally it became too much to bear. To escape the poverty and persecution and pogroms, the Senders, Samuels, Nathans, Abrahams, Dinahs, Solomons, Miriams, began to stream out of the towns of the Pale. They fled to the seacoast cities in western Europe, and with the few rubles they had scraped together, or with money provided by Jewish organizations, they bought steamship tickets to bring them to America. They also came from other countries of Eastern Europe, from Rumania and Hungary. But most of them came from Czarist Russia.

In the year 1881, a year of pogroms, they came in the thousands. The cobblers, tailors, goldsmiths, hatmakers, traders, innkeepers, storekeepers left their towns and fled to the west.

They came again in the thousands in 1882 and in the few years following. For 1882 was the year of the May Laws, when a decree of the Czar uprooted them from hundreds of towns, leaving them homeless.

In 1905, weary of war and starvation and oppression, the Russian people, Jews and Christians alike, joined in revolutionary movements to overthrow the Czar. And again, to direct the attention of the ignorant away from their oppressors, pogroms were organized. The revolutionists did not succeed in overthrowing the Czar, and many of them fled to America to escape persecution. Again Jews came fleeing over the broad highway of the ocean.

For a short time after the first World War, they came

once more, in smaller waves, until, in 1922, Congress passed a law sharply reducing the number of immigrants who might enter America.

Between 1881 and 1922, two million Jews came to the United States from Eastern Europe. During this period, the United States became one of the largest Jewish centers in the world.

The Arrival

When the Russian immigrant arrived in New York City, he felt as though he had stepped into a maze through which he would never find his way. Sometimes there were friends or relatives who had come to the United States before him and who were eager to help him make his way. Often he was helped by organizations set up

STEERAGE PASSENGERS ARRIVING IN NEW YORK HARBOR

principally by the German Jews, who had been in the country for some time. But despite the help the immigrant received, everything seemed vast and strange and new—the bewildering mazes of streets that stretched endlessly in all directions, the crowds of people bustling about, speaking an unfamiliar language, the paved sidewalks and towering buildings, the trolley cars riding on the surface of the ground, the elevated trains riding on tracks high up in the air, the factories, the shops, the policeman in the blue uniform, the public schools for all children, Jews and Christians alike. Looking about him, the immigrant wondered whether he would ever feel at home in the country that had welcomed him to its shores.

But before anything else, the immigrant knew that he must find a home and earn a living. He did not go west to settle on farmland, for the Russian Jewish immigrant was not a farmer. He had often dreamed of owning his own bit of land to plow and sow. But the Czarist government had not permitted him to buy land. He had lived in the crowded towns in Czarist Russia, so he chose the busy, industrial cities of America to live in.

The Russian immigrant made his home in New York City, or in Philadelphia, Boston, Chicago. The Jewish sections of these cities became so crowded that they were often called ghettos. In New York City, a large area known as the lower East Side became the home of hundreds of thousands of Jewish immigrants from Eastern Europe. Whole Russian villages of Jews sometimes found themselves on the same street of the East Side of New York. They opened little synagogues, and people who had lived in the same town in Russia all went to the same synagogue in America. They formed *Landsmanschaften,* or lodges, for mutual aid and for meeting socially.

Most of them wanted to learn English as quickly as possible. Children were sent to public school. The older people went to night school, so that they could learn to read and write and speak the language of their new country. They wanted to make their way quickly, and to learn all they could about the country that had opened its doors to them.

Earning a Living

Earning a living was not easy for the Russian immigrant. America was no longer a land of pioneers, waiting to be developed. The cities, the railroads, the industries had been built. The immigrant was forced to find a place for himself in the large and bustling country.

Sometimes, in his crowded city ghetto, he opened a little grocery or dry-goods store, or he peddled goods from door to door. Some immigrants became shoemakers, hatmakers, tailors. Pushcarts crowded the curbs of the busy lower East Side streets. Behind the pushcarts stood young men and old, selling lace, bits of ribbon, second hand clothes, shoe laces, eye glasses, vegetables, fruit. The pushcart peddlers did not earn enough to keep their families in comfort, but they hoped that their children, some day, would have a better time of it than they did. They dreamt wonderful dreams for their children. They would go to high school, then to college and to the great universities of the country. They would become whatever they pleased—doctors, teachers, professors. They might even be elected to Congress, mused the poor peddler standing behind his pushcart.

In the Factories

Thousands of Russian Jewish immigrants who had been tailors in their old homes entered the clothing factories of New York City, which was the clothing manufacturing center of America. The immigrant sat over his machine for fifteen or sixteen hours a day. And when the working week was over, he found that his pay envelope contained about six or eight dollars. The few dollars he earned had to pay for his rent, food and clothing for the family, doctor bills, and whatever else his family needed. Because there were thousands of men looking for work, the factory owner paid his workers very little. He knew that if a man refused to work for a low salary, he could always get someone else who was eager to find work.

So the immigrant factory worker took what he could get. To increase his earnings, he often brought work home for his wife and children, and they all worked together till the early morning hours so that they could have enough food and warm clothes for the winter.

A worker in the clothing factory did not work all the year round. There was the "slack season," when there was no work for weeks and even months. If a man had some money put aside, it quickly vanished during the slack season, for he still had a family to feed and clothe, though he had no work. Factory workers dreaded the slack season, which meant constant worry about where the food was coming from and how the rent was to be paid.

Sweat Shops

In those days, a sewing machine could be rented for about fifty cents a week. A man might therefore rent a few machines, set them up in the parlor of his little tenement apartment, get a bundle of coats to sew from a coat manufacturer, and hire several immigrants to work for him. When he was paid for the finished garments, he put aside part of the money for the workers he had hired and kept the rest for himself.

The contractor, as this man was called, might get a few more sewing machines, for the more finished garments he delivered to the manufacturer the more money he made. He set the new machines up in his parlor, crowding it till there was barely room to turn around. If things went well, he rented more machines, putting them in the bedroom, in the kitchen, in the dark hallway, even in the cellar. At each machine in these "sweat shops," as the crowded, dark, unsanitary tenement factories were called, sat an immigrant. And each immigrant stitched away from dawn till dark for five, six or eight dollars a week, depending on how much work he turned out.

Labor Unions

In time, the workers in the clothing factories began to organize into unions. They tried to bargain with their employers, asking for higher wages, sanitary conditions, and shorter working days. If bargaining failed, they went out on strike, refusing to return to work till their demands were met.

The strikes were often led by men who had been revolutionists in Russia. They had fought for justice in Russia, seeking to overthrow the Czar, and in America they fought for justice too—decent conditions for the underpaid factory workers. Often, a strike dragged on for months. If a worker had some money saved for a rainy day, it did not last very long. When his savings were gone, there was little or nothing to eat at home. Often a strike would fail, and the disheartened workers found themselves back where they had started from. But gradually, as the unions became larger and stronger, the sweat shops were completely wiped out, and factory owners were forced to raise salaries, shorten the working day, and improve conditions in their factories.

Two of the largest and strongest unions in America,

the Amalgamated Clothing Workers of America and the International Ladies Garment Workers Union, were the work of immigrant Russian Jews on the East Side of New York. By his own efforts, the Jewish immigrant had helped himself and others to a better life.

Old Institutions on New Soil

When the Jewish immigrant came to America from Eastern Europe, he tried to bring with him all that he had cherished in his old home—the synagogue, the Ḥeder, the mutual aid societies, Hebrew—the language of his prayers and his Bible, and Yiddish—the language he spoke. Those who came from the larger cities and who were accustomed to Yiddish newspapers and theaters, tried to establish these too in America.

But what the immigrant brought with him underwent changes in America. In Russia, the Ḥeder was attended by all Jewish boys whose parents were able to pay tuition. For children unable to pay tuition, the community set up the Talmud Torah. When they arrived in America, the Russian Jews at once established Ḥeders for their boys. Jews who had already been in America for many years built Talmud Torahs for the children of immigrants who were unable to pay the tuition of the Ḥeder.

But the Ḥeder could not exist as it had in Russia. The Ḥeder teacher in America was often an uneducated man who could earn a living in no other way but by teaching children to recite their prayers. The lessons were dull and meaningless for the American child. The Talmud Torah, however, had better trained teachers. Its course of studies was richer than that of the Ḥeder. Gradually, the Ḥeder disappeared, and the community Talmud Torah became the accepted Jewish school for the child, for girls as well as boys.

As the Eastern European Jews grew more and more comfortable in their American homes, and as their living conditions improved, many of them left the crowded "ghettos" of the industrial cities and moved to better neighborhoods. When there were enough Jews in a vicinity to form a congregation, they usually built a large, handsome synagogue. But they also needed a Jewish school for their children. Within the synagogue, they set up a school, for boys and girls. This was called a congregational school, and in time it began to replace some of the Talmud Torahs.

The Jewish communities grew larger and synagogues and schools increased in number. Then the people set up bureaus of Jewish education to help and guide the Jewish schools of the city. The bureaus helped organize the schools, helped work out the curriculum, and if there were problems, helped the schools solve them.

Like the schools, the newspapers also underwent changes in America. The Yiddish newspaper which the immigrant bought on the newsstand on his way to work, gave him world news, articles on American history, current events, fiction stories, poetry, political and religious discussions. The immigrant had once known only the small town of the Pale. Now a wide new world was spread before him in his Yiddish newspaper.

Authors who had written in Hebrew in Russia continued to write Hebrew books and poetry in America.

oppressed them. Knowing how the Russian government had always mistreated its Jewish subjects, the Russian High Command feared that the Jews would welcome the enemy armies with joy and even give them help. So it happened, time and again, that the Russian High Command ordered thousands of Jews to move east, into the interior of Russia. It did not matter that the Jews had no place to go, nor that many would die on the way. They were packed like cattle into cars and deported, sometimes as far as Siberia.

Back and forth went the armies, and the Jews did not know who their friends were and who their enemies. Jewish refugees roamed the highways of Russia and Poland. In the thousands, they wandered about, seeking food and shelter.

The End of the Czars

For many years, the Czarist government had been toppling. The people were poor, oppressed, with nothing to look forward to but continued poverty. In 1917, when millions of Russians had grown weary of war and hunger, the government fell at last, and Nicholas II, the last Czar of Russia, was forced to abdicate. Revolution broke with fury over Russia. The government passed into the hands of the Bolsheviks, who brought many changes to Russia.

Some of the changes affected the Jews of that country. One of the laws the Bolsheviks passed made anti-Semitism a criminal offense. For the first time in their history in Russia, the Jews were granted complete civil and political equality. The Bolsheviks, however, were opposed to religion of any kind. They were also opposed to Zionism. Because of this, Judaism, as it had existed for centuries in Russia, as a religion and as a way of life, began gradually to disappear.

For a long time after the revolution, confusion reigned, as often happens after a revolution. In the confusion, armies tramped back and forth over the districts of the Eastern Front. Some of these armies were merely bands of men who wanted to bring back the reign of the Czar. They fell in fury upon the Jews, blaming them for the revolution. Again thousands of Jews became refugees, roaming the highways and seeking shelter in the forests. Again pogroms broke out, claiming almost a half million Jews among the dead.

Uniting to Help

The Jews of America were roused by the suffering of their people in Eastern Europe. The news that trickled into America told of looting, killing, homelessness, starvation. People heard of their home towns wiped from the face of the earth. They looked in vain for news of parents or friends who had remained in Eastern Europe. *Landsmanschaften* sent whatever money they could gather for food, clothing, shelter.

Committees too were established to help the Jews of Eastern Europe. In 1906, after the massacre of many Jews in Kishineff, a city in Russia, the American Jewish

The First World War

Committee was established. Another committee was organized in 1914, to help Orthodox Jews in Eastern Europe. Then came another committee, organized by Jewish workers, to collect funds for Jewish workers who had suffered the miseries of the war.

Different committees meant helping some Jews and discriminating against others. It also meant waste of time and money, and less efficiency in reaching the war victims. It was not long before the three committees joined ranks. They called themselves the Joint Distribution Committee, or the JDC. The JDC decided that all the money collected by the different committees would go into one treasury, and help would go to all Jews who needed it, regardless of whether they were Orthodox,

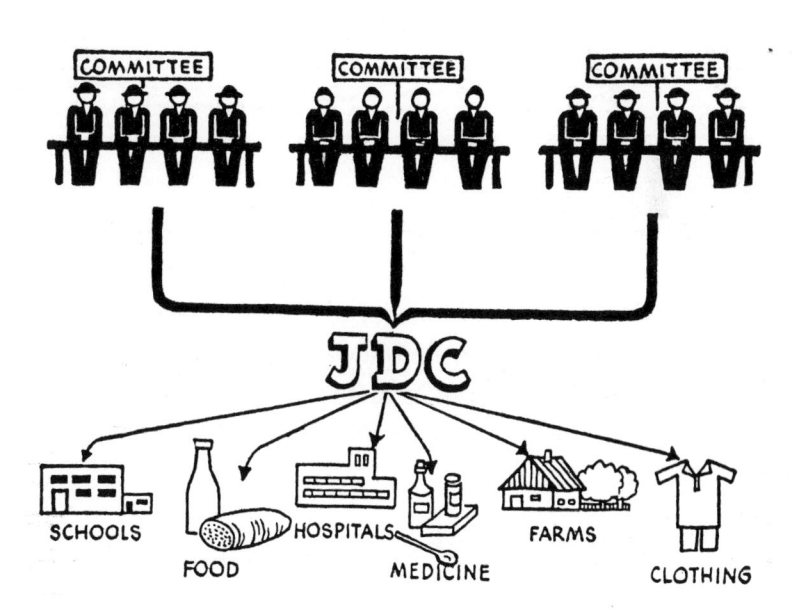

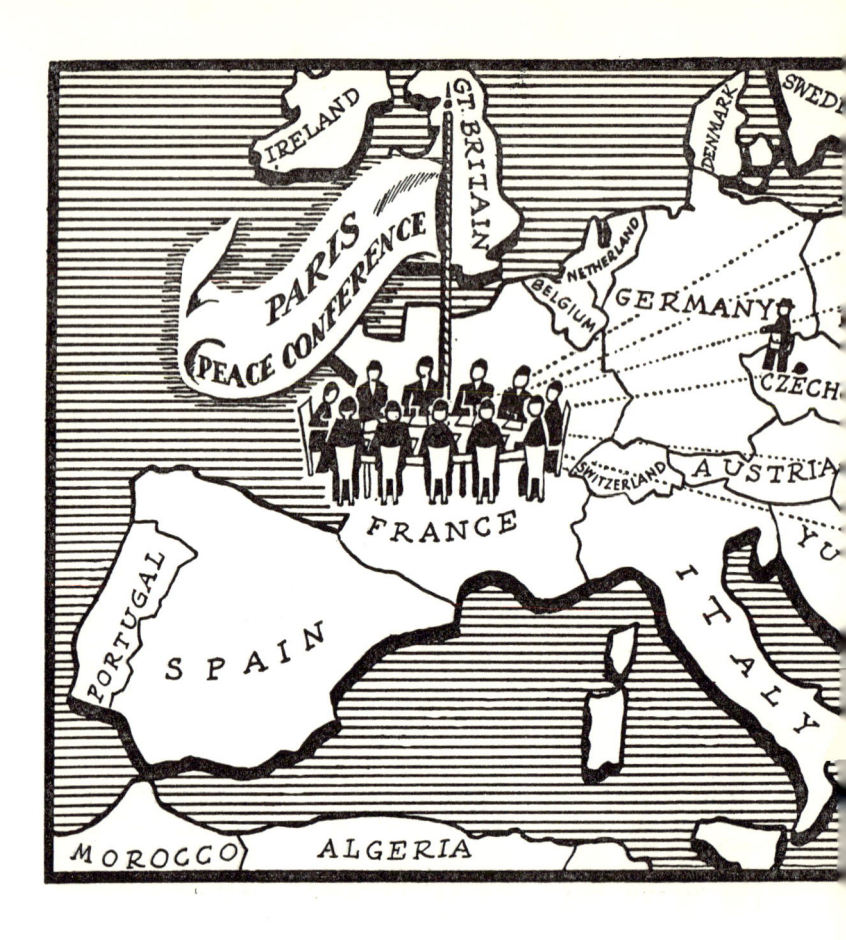

Zionist or worker, and regardless of where the money came from.

Year after year, millions of dollars flowed into the treasury of the JDC. The money went overseas for food, clothing, medicine, hospitals, schools, and for helping Jews who had never been farmers settle on the soil.

The Peace Conference

Peace came on November 11, 1918. The heads of the

COUNTRIES IN WHICH RIGHTS OF MINORITIES WERE GUARANTEED PROTECTION

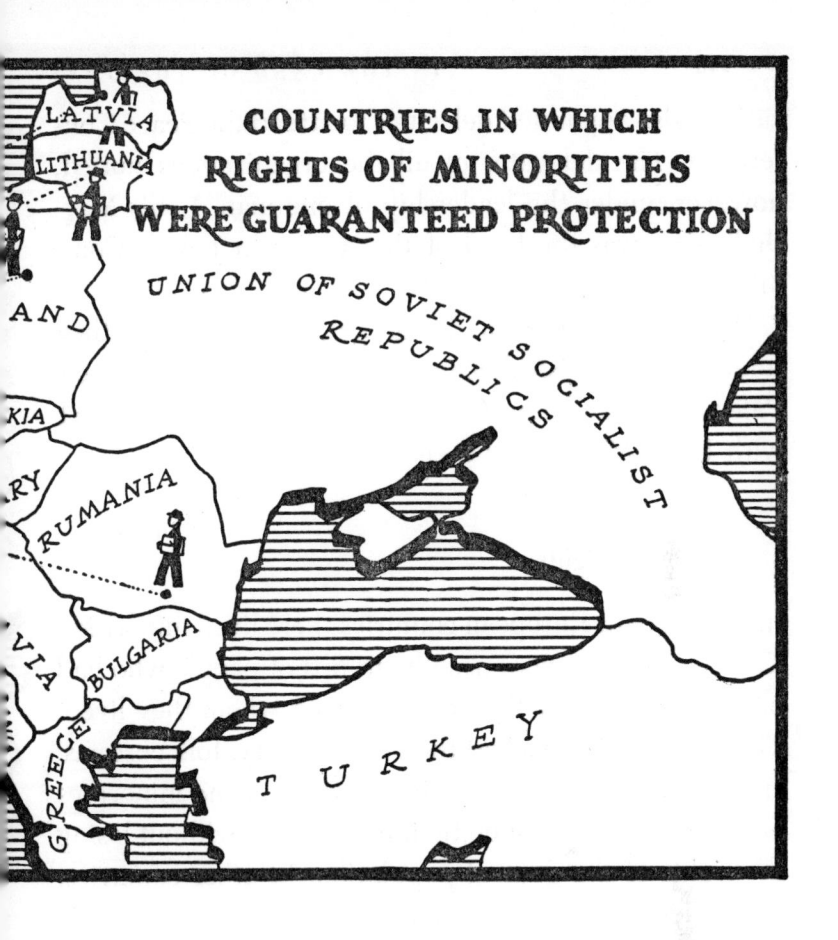

victorious nations decided to meet in Paris to discuss the future of Europe. Jews everywhere felt that they had been victims of prejudice and tyranny long enough. They wanted their rights protected by the nations of the world.

In America, a movement began to elect an American Jewish Congress which would send delegates to represent the Jews of America at the Peace Conference. Three-hundred-thousand Jews voted for their delegates to the American Jewish Congress. The Congress, in turn, chose delegates to go to Paris. Several other Jewish organizations also appointed delegates to attend the Peace Conference. The delegates of all the organizations united, however, under the leadership of one man, Louis Marshall, who was the head of the American Jewish Committee.

When the American delegation reached Paris, they found other Jewish delegations, from England, France, Palestine, Poland, East Galicia. The delegations all united, with Louis Marshall as their chairman.

Minority Rights

In a number of European countries there lived minorities. These minorities were usually groups of people who had been conquered by the people among whom they lived. The minority groups had their own history, folk customs, and often religion. In certain countries, some minorities had the right to continue their cultural life without losing the rights of the general population. In other countries, minorities were not protected.

In most of the Central and East European countries, there were Jewish minority groups. They too were eager to have their minority rights—the right to their own schools, customs, religion—at the same time enjoying the civil and political rights of the general population.

The Jewish delegation presented to the Peace Conference a plan for minority rights for the Jews. According to their plan, the Jewish minorities in the East European countries were to be permitted their own customs, schools, religion, language. At the same time, they were not to lose the political and civil rights which the population as a whole enjoyed.

The Peace Conference accepted the plan worked out by the Jewish delegation. The League of Nations guaranteed minority rights not only to the Jews, but to other minorities as well. In the peace treaties drawn up for Poland, Rumania, Czechoslovakia, Lithuania, Latvia, and Hungary, the members of minorities were guaranteed protection by their governments, and if this failed, by the League of Nations. In defending their own rights at the Peace Conference, the Jews were defending the rights of all minorities.

Looking Forward

The first World War brought changes to many people of the world. The hated Czar of Russia was overthrown and a government came to power which promised equality to all its inhabitants. Minorities in a number of European countries were guaranteed their rights. In Germany, the kaiser was overthrown and a democratic republic was set up. The Jews of America had developed into a strong and independent community. As we shall see in the following chapters, the dream of the Zionists for a Jewish homeland in Palestine was also about to come true.

On the surface, the future seemed bright. But clouds were gathering, even as the delegates of the League of Nations sat around the peace table in Paris. And it was not long before the clouds burst, and a storm such as mankind had never seen broke over the world.

For the Pupil

THINGS TO READ:

Leonard, Oscar, *Americans All,* "He Charley McCarthy'd Them," page 216, "He Saved the Lost Battalion," page 221.

THINGS TO TALK ABOUT:

1. Why was it wise for the Jewish delegations to the Peace Conference to join ranks?
2. Why were the Jews of America able to take on the task of helping their people overseas?

THINGS TO DO:

Write to the JDC for material on the work they are doing today. Discuss the material they send you.

Teacher's Bibliography

Grayzel, Solomon, *A History of the Jews,* pp. 712-721.
Learsi, Rufus, *Israel,* pp. 571-576.

UNIT SIX

The Rebirth of Israel

*And I will turn the captivity of My people Israel,
And they shall build the waste cities, and inhabit them;
And they shall plant vineyards, and drink the wine
	thereof;
They shall also make gardens, and eat the fruit of them.
And I will plant them upon their land,
And they shall no more be plucked up
Out of their land which I have given them,
Saith the Lord thy God.*
(Amos, 9:14-15)

CHAPTER ONE

Pioneers in Palestine

Palestine Since the Destruction of the Temple

In the year 70, when Jerusalem was conquered by Rome, the second Jewish Commonwealth came to an end. Many Jews were killed by the Romans. Many were sold into slavery. Thousands fled to other lands.

Gradually, the little land which the Bible had called a land of milk and honey, became a land of desolation. The waves of the sea came sweeping over the shoreline. For years the waves swept back and forth, washing up the sands of the sea. Year by year the sands mounted, swept in by winds and waves, till lonely sand dunes stretched over miles of coastland. And inland, the orchards and vineyards, with no one to care for them, fell into decay. City walls crumbled, and fields lay parched under the hot sun.

As time went by, the land grew more and more impoverished, and the Jewish population grew smaller. Old empires vanished. Rome was defeated by a stronger power and Palestine passed into new hands. When the Mohammedans conquered Palestine and other lands of the East, Arabs settled in Palestine. Again and again, through the ages, Palestine passed from one conqueror to the next, until finally it became the possession of the Turkish empire.

Still Palestine slumbered on. Swamps formed over pastureland that had once been green and over fields that had bloomed with wheat and barley and rye. And in ancient cities crumbling with age, a handful of Jewish cobblers and weavers and dyers bent to their work, dreaming of the glory that had passed.

New Dwellers of Palestine

From surrounding lands, from Egypt, Arabia, Syria, Lebanon, Iraq, Transjordan, Arabs drifted in and settled on the few fertile spots of Palestine. Much of the land passed into the hands of rich Arab owners, who leased it out to Arab peasants. The peasants were poor, living as their forefathers had lived, in huts of baked mud. Their primitive plows scratched the surface of the soil, which yielded barely enough grain to supply their needs. The women wove and spun coarse cloth of camels hair, and they ground their grain between two stones, as their mothers had done before them. Though the Arab peasants had barely enough to eat, they paid heavy taxes and rent to the wealthy Arab landlords, who lived in luxurious homes, often in distant cities.

Going Up

Late in the nineteenth century, a movement to return to Zion had begun among the Jews of Europe. The persecution by the Czars of Russia had sent large waves of Jews across the ocean to America, while a small trickle went east, to Palestine. In 1882 came a group of pioneers, the BILU, to build a life of freedom in the ancient homeland. The first *Aliyah*, this was called, the first "going up." The pioneers had been city and town dwellers in Europe, and they longed for the freedom of open fields and the outdoor life of the farmer. They knew that the land of their dreams had turned into malarial swamps and barren fields. But they were ready to work for the life they had dreamed of in their little villages and towns. Many of them died of the diseases that ravaged the land. But the survivors drained swamps and planted fields and built homes, blazing the trail for others.

The second *Aliyah* brought thousands of new settlers to Palestine. It began in 1905 and continued till 1914, when the First World War broke out. As more and more Jews arrived to drain the swampland and break through the stony soil, the little land began to wake from its long slumber.

The pioneers, or *Halutzim*, of the second *Aliyah* were not happy with the kind of life the pioneers of the first *Aliyah* had built. The pioneers of the first *Aliyah* had returned to the soil, as they had wanted to do, and they had become successful farmers, with Arab peasants working for them.

But the new pioneers did not want a society where one man worked for another. They wanted all men working together, in one community, all sharing equally the fruit of their labors.

Cooperative Settlements

So the pioneers of the second *Aliyah* built different types of cooperative settlements. These settlements were developed on land bought from the Arabs by the Jewish National Fund, a Zionist organization which bought land in Palestine in the name of the Jewish people.

The most important of the new types of settlements was the *Kibbutz*, a complete cooperative. Though the *Halutzim* worked and lived on the land, they did not own it, for it belonged to all the Jews as a people. No one in a *Kibbutz* worked for anyone else. All the pioneers worked together, some plowing, some building, some gardening, some taking care of the livestock.

The *Kibbutz* became the new way of life for many

people in Palestine. In the coming years, many new *Kibbutzim* developed, each with its school, orchards, gardens, dairies, chickens, livestock. The money the settlers earned when they sold their surplus products went into improving the *Kibbutz*. They bought more livestock, tractors, harvesters, school equipment—whatever the settlers needed to improve the life of their settlement.

Histadrut

One of the most important accomplishments of the pioneers of the second *Aliyah* was the building of *Histadrut Haovdim*, the General Federation of Labor. This organization, which became the backbone of Palestine, was founded in the early days of the second *Aliyah*. The *Histadrut* was an organization of all working people not employing others—union members, co-operative farmers, professionals. As the *Histadrut* grew stronger, it established hospitals, clinics, rest homes, unemployment insurance, loan societies, schools for the children. Engineering enterprises, and even the running of basic industries like building and the manufacture of steel, became part of the program of *Histadrut*. Today, about half the people of Palestine are affiliated with *Histadrut*.

Hadassah

In 1909, an American woman, Henrietta Szold, came to visit Palestine. She saw the diseases from which so many of the people suffered. Diseases often went unchecked, for there were few doctors and nurses in Palestine to teach the people the rules of hygiene.

When Henrietta Szold returned to America, she founded Hadassah, the Women's Zionist Organization. Hadassah made it its work to bring health to Palestine. At first Hadassah could send only a few nurses to work among a population suffering from trachoma, malaria, and other tropical diseases. But as Hadassah's membership grew, it built hospitals and clinics and child-care centers. Arabs and Jews alike enjoyed the benefits of Hadassah's health program. The hospitals, clinics and health centers were open to all. Visiting nurses taught mothers how to care for their children. Hygiene was taught in the schools. Slowly the knowledge of hygiene spread, and some of the diseases from which many Arabs and Jews had suffered almost disappeared.

The Balfour Declaration

In 1914 came the First World War, with England fighting as one of the Allies. In ancient days, Palestine had been the bridge connecting great empires. Now, too, Palestine was the bridge leading into larger and richer lands. But Palestine was still in the hands of Turkey, which was fighting on the side of Germany.

One of England's aims in the war was to win Palestine, the gateway to Egypt, Syria, and other lands of the Mediterranean region. If England won Palestine, it would be to her benefit to have within the land a population friendly to the English government. Among the general population of England, there had been a feeling, for many years, that Palestine should be the homeland of the Jewish people. The time had come, Zionist leaders felt, for negotiations with Britain to make Palestine Israel's homeland.

There lived in England, at this time, the World Zionist leader, the man who was one day to become the first president of the new State of Israel, Dr. Chaim Weizmann. Dr. Weizmann was a chemist, and he taught chem-

DR. CHAIM WEIZMANN

istry at Manchester University. It happened that Chaim Weizmann developed a new formula for acetone, which was an important ingredient in the manufacture of explosives. His discovery brought Weizmann closer to English statesmen directing the war. He often discussed with Lord Balfour and other statesmen the meaning of Palestine to thousands of Jews, and the importance to England of a Palestine with a friendly Jewish population.

Discussions went on for months, other Zionist leaders working with Weizmann in the negotiations for Palestine. Finally, on November 2, 1917, Great Britain issued a statement known as the Balfour Declaration.

> His Majesty's Government view with favor the establishment in Palestine of a national home for the Jewish people, and will use their best endeavors to facilitate the achievement

of this object, it being clearly understood that nothing shall be done which may prejudice the civil and religious rights of existing non-Jewish communities in Palestine or the rights and political status enjoyed by Jews in any other country.

To Jews the world over it seemed that a miracle had taken place. After almost two thousand years, Palestine was again to be the homeland of the Jewish people. It had happened before, in the year 538 B.C.E., when Cyrus, the king of Persia, had issued a proclamation permitting the Jews who had been exiled to Babylonia to return to their homeland. Now again, in 1917, those who wished could return to the land where they had once lived as a nation.

On Mount Scopus

On November 11, nine days after the Balfour Declaration had startled the Jews of the world, General Allenby marched into Jerusalem with his troops. He entered the Holy City not as a conqueror, but as a pilgrim, his head uncovered.

Eight months later, in July, 1918, an assembly gathered on Mount Scopus in the city of Jerusalem to lay the cornerstone of a Hebrew University. Far in the distance could be heard the sound of gunfire as the Turkish troops still fought the British. But for the men and women assembled on Mount Scopus the sounds of war were over, and only the future stretched before them, with its promise of freedom and peace. Hundreds of years back, the exiles returning to Palestine from Babylonia had assembled to build an altar for their Temple, which was to be the central house of worship for Jews in every land. Now their descendants, in 1918, laid a cornerstone for a University which they hoped would be a great house of learning not only for the Jews of Palestine, but for the Jews of all the world.

For the Pupil

THINGS TO READ:

Read the declaration of Cyrus in your copy of the Jewish Publication Society Bible, Book of Ezra, page 1027, chapter I, verses 2 through 4.

THINGS TO TALK ABOUT:

1. Compare the Cyrus Declaration and the Balfour Declaration.
2. Why was it easier for the pioneers of the second *Aliyah* to build cooperatives than it was for the pioneers of the first *Aliyah?*
3. Why do we compare the building of the altar with the laying of the cornerstone for a university in the city of Jerusalem? Why were both these events unusual in the life of pioneers?
4. What did the first *Aliyah* contribute to the development of Palestine? What did the second *Aliyah* contribute?

THINGS TO DO:

1. Write to Hadassah for material on its work in Palestine. See if you can use some of this material for your scrapbook on Palestine.
2. Write to the Zionist Organization of America asking whether you may borrow some movies on Palestine suitable for your class.

Teacher's Bibliography

Bardin, Solomon, *Pioneer Youth in Palestine*, Bloch Publishing Co., 1932.

Edidin, Ben M., *Rebuilding of Palestine*, Behrman Book House, 1939.

Grayzel, Solomon, *A History of the Jews*, pp. 717-719.

Learsi, Rufus, *Israel*, pp. 551-553; 576-582.

Samuel, Maurice, *Harvest in the Desert*, Jewish Publication Society, 1944.

THE HEBREW UNIVERSITY
ON MT. SCOPUS, JERUSALEM

CHAPTER TWO

ᨆ Between Two Wars

Building the Land

The Balfour Declaration, with its promise of a homeland for the Jewish people, brought thousands of new settlers to Palestine. The barren land grew green and fertile as the pioneers irrigated the parched soil and put it to the plow. Bit by bit Palestine began to bustle with new life. In 1925, the Hebrew University opened on Mount Scopus. The Valley of Jezreel was drained and plowed and planted, so that it bloomed again as it had bloomed in Biblical days. Tel-Aviv, which the pioneers had built as a suburb of Jaffa upon a stretch of lonely sand dunes, became one of the most modern cities of the mid-Eastern world. The pioneers had hoped it would be a beautiful garden city, but so rapidly did the population grow that it became the largest city in Palestine, with restaurants, cafés, apartment houses, concert halls, theatres, factories. Modern suburbs grew up around Jerusalem, the Holy City, outside the old fortress walls. The new section of Jerusalem became the "New City," with apartment houses, public buildings, schools, industry, crafts. The old city of Haifa, nestling at the foot of Mount Carmel, developed into a modern city, one of the most beautiful

THE NEW CITY OF JERUSALEM

in Palestine. New houses were built and gardens were cultivated on the slopes of Mount Carmel, overlooking the sea. The port of Haifa became one of the most important ports of the Eastern Mediterranean, while the bay area became the industrial center of Palestine.

The Arab Peasant and the Jewish Farmer

But many rich Arab landowners did not want to see Palestine become the Jewish national homeland. They did not want to see a flourishing society, where there were no landowners who lived on the labors of peasant tenants. Side by side with the Arab peasants lived the Jewish farmer in his collective settlement. The poor Arab, in his hut of baked mud, saw his Jewish neighbors enjoy the benefits of tractors and harvesters. He saw their fertile fields, their trim, sanitary cottages, their healthy livestock, their rich orchards of fruit. The Arab landlords feared that the Arab peasant might learn new ideas from his Jewish neighbors and long for the richer life he saw around him.

There were other Arabs too who did not want Palestine to become the Jewish national homeland. Among the younger, educated Arabs, a feeling of nationalism was awakening. These Arabs wanted Palestine to be not a Jewish, but an Arab state.

The Island in the Arab World

There were also many English officials who were opposed to the Jewish life developing in Palestine. In the vast Arab world of Syria, Transjordan, Egypt, Iraq, Arabia, there lived millions and millions of Arabs, obedient to their Arab rulers and to the British officials. The Jewish population in Palestine was but a small island in the vast Arab world. Would it not be better, thought many British officials and statesmen, to win the friendship of the Arabs, who were so much more numerous than the Jews? Friendship with influential Arabs might mean, for England, winning rights to the Arabian oil wells. Oil was important for English industry, and for war, if another war should come.

Also, English merchants and manufacturers could sell their products to Arab countries, which had developed no machinery for manufacturing their own products. But the Jews were not a backward people, ready to serve as a market for whatever products England wished to sell them. The Jewish population in Palestine was developing industry, as well as the soil. The Jews were an independent people, developing their own democratic way of life. And so to many British officials, as well as to many Arabs, it seemed best that Palestine should not be permitted to develop as the Jewish homeland.

The White Paper

After the war, the British government had received from the League of Nations the Mandate for Palestine. This meant that Palestine belonged to the League of Nations, and that it was to be managed for the League of Nations by Great Britain. It meant also that Palestine was under the protection of the British, who were to keep peace in the land.

But there was no peace in Palestine. Some Arab leaders sent agents among the peasants to tell them strange tales about their Jewish neighbors. It was the Jews, the peasants were told, who were responsible for their poverty. The Jews, said the agents, would take over the Mohammedan holy places, and gradually, they would destroy the Mohammedan religion.

Believing all they heard, many Arab peasants let themselves be led into riots against the Jewish settlements. In 1920, in 1921, and again in 1929, Jews and Arabs alike were killed in the riots which raged over Palestine, now in one section of the land, and now in another.

Hoping to win the friendship of the Arabs, and using the riots as the reason for stopping Jewish immigration into Palestine, the British government issued, shortly after the riots of 1929, what is known as the White Paper.

The White Paper not only reduced the quota of Jews entering Palestine each year, but it also stated that the Jewish National Fund could buy no more land from the Arabs.

Self-Defense

But so great were the protests against the White Paper, even by members of the British Parliament, that it was soon withdrawn. Immigration continued, and the *Yishuv*, as the Jewish community of Palestine was called, continued to grow.

To protect the land and the people against Arab rioters, thousands of young men and women organized themselves into a secret self-defense organization, called *Haganah*. Members of *Haganah* defended the settlements when they were attacked. They guarded workmen on their way to the factories. They did not return terror for terror. They adopted the policy of *Havlagah,* which means self discipline, fighting only in self-defense. The work of the *Haganah* was to defend the people and what the people were building in Palestine.

Developing the Yishuv

In the meantime, the work of the pioneers continued to transform the little land into a flowering garden and an industrial center. Trucks loaded with vegetables and eggs and poultry rumbled along the roads to the busy city markets. The waters of the Jordan River were harnessed and their power used for electricity in homes and factories. Potash and other minerals were extracted from the Dead Sea and used in industry. The Jewish National Fund planted trees on the slopes of hills to hold down the soil. Trees were also planted to drain marshes and swamps.

Even parts of the wildernesses, untouched by man for hundreds of years, came to life. In the very midst of hostile territory, pioneers would arrive in the dead of night, and on an uncultivated section of land they would erect a water tower ringed by barricades. Arabs gazed in amazement when they awoke in the morning and found a settlement where there had been only tangled shrubs. While guards patrolled the new settlement, the work within the barricades went on day and night. Shacks to serve as temporary homes were quickly erected. A common dining room was built. Electricity and water pipes were installed. And soon tractors moved over the fields as a new section of wilderness was reclaimed by the pioneers.

Hebrew Culture Reborn

Together with the factories and the settlements, Hebrew culture developed. The Hebrew language became the spoken language of the land, for the pioneers had determined that, with the soil, they would also revive the Hebrew language.

Reviving Hebrew as a spoken language is usually associated with Eliezer ben Yehudah, who was the first to insist on using Hebrew as his everyday language. Eliezer ben Yehudah came to Palestine in 1881, when it was but a land of sandy wastes and marshes. Before entering Jerusalem, the city where he settled, Eliezer ben Yehudah vowed that he would speak only Hebrew. His neighbors were horrified when they heard Hebrew, the sacred language of the Bible, used by ben Yehudah and his wife in everyday speech. But Eliezer ben Yehudah and his wife paid no attention to their neighbors, and when a child was born to them, they spoke only Hebrew to the child. It happened that the child was slow in learning to speak, and ben Yehudah's superstitious neighbors said that here was the hand of God, punishing them through their child for profaning the holy tongue. But at last the child spoke, and his first words were Hebrew words.

For forty years, Eliezer ben Yehudah worked on a gigantic Hebrew dictionary which was to contain every Hebrew word that existed, old and new. If there were no Hebrew words to describe an object, an action or an idea, ben Yehudah coined new words.

Gradually, Eliezer ben Yehudah won his long and lonely battle. Hebrew slowly became the everyday language of the land. In the schools of the cities and settlements, children studied in the Hebrew language. Plays were written and acted in Hebrew. New songs were sung in the language of the Hebrew prophets. The little newsboy on the corner of a street in Tel-Aviv hawked his papers in Hebrew. Hebrew art, Hebrew books, a new Hebrew culture developed wherever the pioneers came to build.

The Rise of the Nazis

Germany and her allies had lost the First World War. As a vanquished nation, Germany had to pay reparations to the victorious nations. In addition, prices were high in postwar Germany, and the wages workers received were low. The war had been costly for most of the Germans, leaving them poor and discouraged. Germany was an impoverished, dissatisfied country, smarting under the shame of defeat.

There was a large group of people in Germany who believed that they were a "master race," a nation whose destiny it was to rule the world. The shame they felt at having lost the war made their desire to rule the world stronger than ever.

In 1933 Adolph Hitler came to power, for he promised the German people a great and rich future. The republic set up in Germany after the war was overthrown, and

Hitler became the *fuehrer,* or leader, of the German people.

Hitler and his followers, who were called Nazis, ruled Germany with brutality and terror. They silenced all those who opposed their reign with murder, or with imprisonment in concentration camps. Thousands of men and women were killed as the Nazis tightened their hold on the German people.

Like many oppressors before them, the Nazis used the Jews as a scapegoat, saying that they were responsible for Germany's defeat and poverty. The Jews, they said, were an "inferior race," as well as the enemies of Germany. So thousands of Jews in Germany were driven from their stores, their shops, and from the universities and the professions. They were thrown into prison, robbed, reduced to poverty. No one dared defend the Jews, for defending the Jews meant death.

The Nazis grew stronger and stronger as German munition factories turned out instruments of war. Then began the push of the Nazis to conquer Europe, the first step toward conquering the world. They marched into Austria, Czechoslovakia, Poland. Wherever they went, they brought terror to those who opposed them, and to those whom they considered their enemies.

The Second World War

In 1939 the Second World War began. In time, many countries, among them Britain, France, the United States and Soviet Russia, were drawn into the war against the Nazis. During the war, the Nazis began to murder the

Jews of Germany and of the countries they had conquered. The people who called themselves "super-men" and the "master race" murdered six million Jews, the worst slaughter in the history of the world.

In 1939, after three years of Arab riots, and in the very year the war broke out, Great Britain issued a White Paper which sharply reduced Jewish immigration into Palestine. When thousands of Jews, fleeing death by the Nazis, were trying to reach Palestine, the British government closed the doors of that country, leaving them to their fate. For now more than ever Britain wanted the friendship of the Arabs. Britain feared that the Arabs might help the Nazis, as some of their leaders were already doing. Britain was sure of the loyalty of the Jews in the fight against the common enemy, the Nazis. But not being sure of the Arabs, she did whatever she could to appease them and win them to her side.

But the Jews of Palestine determined to fight both the Nazis and the White Paper, for both were their enemies. "We will fight beside Great Britain," declared the Zionist Congress which met in Geneva just before the outbreak of the war, "as though there were no White Paper, and we will fight the White Paper as though there were no war."

༄༅ For the Pupil

THINGS TO READ:

1. Lurie, Rose, *The Great March,* Book Two, "Lost! A Hundred Dollars," page 190.
2. Pessin, Deborah, *Michael Turns the Globe,* "Hanita," page 122.
3. Pessin, Deborah, *Giants on the Earth,* "The Dreamer," page 62.

THINGS TO TALK ABOUT:

1. Why did rich Arab landowners feel themselves threatened by a developing Jewish homeland in Palestine?
2. Why did the *Haganah* adopt the policy of *Havlagah?*
3. Why did Palestine develop so rapidly?

THINGS TO DO:

1. Arrange a Palestine exhibit. See how many articles you can bring from home or borrow from relatives.
2. Make an animated map showing some of the industries of Palestine. Put in some of the most famous cities and settlements of Palestine. If you do not have enough material on hand, write to the Jewish National Fund, asking for the kind of material you need.

༄༅ Teacher's Bibliography

Berges, Max, *Cold Pogrom,* J.P.S., 1939.

Edidin, Ben M., *Rebuilding Palestine,* Behrman House, 1939.

Grayzel, Solomon, *A History of the Jews,* pp. 759-766.

Learsi, Rufus, *Israel,* pp. 591-650.

CHAPTER THREE

∿∿ Resistance and War

Fighting the War

When the Second World War broke out, the Jews of Palestine united to fight the Nazis and their allies. Palestine was not officially in the war and her men could not be drafted. Yet the Jewish Agency, the unofficial governing body of the *Yishuv*, set up registration stations and called for volunteers. Thousands of men and women responded, many of them volunteering to fight in Britain's armies.

The Jewish soldiers in Britain's armies fought the Nazis in France, Italy, Crete, Malta, North Africa, Abyssinia. But they wanted an army of their own, led by their own commander and carrying their own flag. It was not till late in the war, however, that Britain permitted them to form their own brigade and to fight as a distinct group. Led by a Jewish commander, marching behind their own banners, and with the insignia of the Star of David on their shoulders, soldiers of the *Yishuv* were able at last to fight hand to hand with the enemies of freedom.

On the Home Front

On the home front, too, the *Yishuv* mobilized for war. The farms stepped up production. The food the people ate was rationed, so that large supplies could go to the allied armies stationed in Palestine and in neighboring countries. New factories were opened to turn out materials needed in the war. Medical supplies, surgical instruments, serums, vaccines, drugs, were produced and sent to the front line stations. Roads, camps, fortifications were built by thousands of men working day and night.

Resistance

In every country conquered by Germany, resistance movements were organized to fight the Nazis and to help their victims. The resistance groups worked secretly, disrupting enemy plans, helping prisoners escape, smuggling victims of the Nazis to safety. Jewish children in occupied France were sometimes smuggled over the border by groups of Christian boy scouts, who pretended they were merely out for a stroll over the countryside. In Holland, Jews were often hidden in Christian homes. Men would go out on a dark night and dynamite railroad tracks used by the Nazis. German planes would suddenly go up in flames. Sentries were ambushed and killed. In factories manufacturing arms for the Germans, something would suddenly go wrong with the machinery.

Partisan, or resistance groups roamed the forests, or worked underground in the cities. Wherever they could, Jews joined the underground resistance movement, and often they formed their own resistance groups within the underground movement. In France, a Jewish group of resistance fighters captured a trainload of German soldiers. As the Germans surrendered and their captors boarded the train, every Jew shouted into the face of the enemy, *"Ich bin Jude!"* ("I am a Jew!") In the forests of Poland, Jewish groups waylaid and killed many Germans as, toward the end of the war, they came fleeing out of Russia.

The Warsaw Ghetto

The story of the resistance movement against the Nazis is the story of the human spirit in its struggle against evil. One of the brightest episodes in this long story is about the Jews in the Warsaw ghetto.

When the Nazis came to Poland, they herded 450,000 Jews into the Warsaw ghetto. In October, 1940, they put brick walls and barbed wire around the ghetto, so that the Jews would be completely cut off from the outside world. The plan of the Nazis was to wipe out the Jews in the ghetto by May, 1943.

Hunger and disease took their toll of many Jewish lives. But the Jews had determined that they would not let their spirit be broken by the Nazis. They planted green plants on the window sills of their crowded rooms. They organized nurseries for their children. They ran concerts and art exhibitions. They wrote poetry and published newspapers. They intensified their Jewish studies. Their scholars wrote records of what they were doing, hiding the records for future generations to find.

The Nazis, anxious to break the morale of the Jews, murdered their orchestra leaders, their outstanding scholars, their artists. But others took their place, though they knew that their turn would come next. They were ordinary people, the Jews of the ghetto. They did not consider themselves heroes. Yet they were not afraid to face death, for they felt that in their defiance they were protecting the honor of their people. Even in death, they triumphed over their executioners, who had failed to break their spirit.

In the summer of 1942, the Nazis felt that they must speed up the murder of their victims. Each day they sent thousands of Jews to be killed in the gas chambers of Treblinka. By the spring of 1943, there were only forty thousand Jews left of the original 450,000.

Then an amazing thing happened. The prisoners of the ghetto, fenced in by brick walls and barbed wire, rose up against their murderers. In preparation for their last defense, they had secretly built bunkers and had fortified areas of the ghetto. Small arms had been smuggled in. The various organizations had been unified into the Jewish Fighting Organization. Men and women, most of them young, had been assigned posts and duties. When the Nazis came into the ghetto, one morning, to seize the remaining Jews and send them off to the gas chambers, a pitched battle took place, and the Nazis, despite their superior arms, were forced to retreat.

As the Jewish Fighting Organization waited for the next battle, they strengthened their fortifications and built tunnels reaching to the ghetto walls.

Then the Nazis came, this time in the thousands, with machine guns, tanks, and trucks filled with ammunition. The Jewish defenders knew that they could not win the battle, but before they died, they determined that they would kill as many Nazis as they could. The young men and women stationed themselves at their posts in each house and opened fire on their enemies. The Nazis advanced, house by house, street by street, paying dearly for each Jewish defender who fell at his post.

The fighting went on for a month. Less and less did the Nazis wish to fight the Jews hand to hand, for never had they encountered such stubborn resistance and such fierce defiance. One dying Jewish fighter had mocked them from a balcony. Another Jew nonchalantly played melodies from Beethoven and Schubert on his harmonica. The spirit of the defenders seemed stronger than ever.

Finally, the Nazis decided to carry on the battle from the air and from tanks, so that they would not have to fight the Jews at close range. Bombs were rained down on the ghetto and the houses were put to flame. Bloodhounds were used to track down the survivors in the secret bunkers. And finally, the last Jewish gun was silenced, many fighters keeping their last bullets for themselves and their families. A few Jews managed to escape through the underground tunnels, making their way to the forests where they joined other underground groups.

The Warsaw ghetto was burned to the ground. But the glory of its defenders resounded through the world, filling others with courage to defend civilization against barbarism.

"Blessed Is the Match"

Among the most heroic of the fighters from Palestine were the parachutists who let themselves be dropped behind enemy lines on the European continent. The parachutists were a small group of young people, trained by British officers. Their task was not only to help the resistance movement and to act as Intelligence Agents for the British, but also to rescue as many Jews as they could.

One of the parachutists was young Hanna Senesch, who wrote a poem describing the contentment she felt with the dangerous work she had chosen. Her work, she said, was as the work of a match which kindles a flame. With the kindling of the flame the match is consumed, but the flame burns on.

> Blessed is the match that is consumed in kindling flame.
> Blessed is the flame that burns in the secret fastness of the heart.
> Blessed is the heart with strength to stop its beating for honor's sake.
> Blessed is the match that is consumed in kindling flame.
> (Translation by Marie Syrkin)

Hanna Senesch, a wealthy girl in Hungary, had dreamed of living as a *Halutzah* in Palestine. Hanna was eighteen years old when her dream came true and she sailed for Palestine. It seemed then, to the young pioneer, that a peaceful and happy life stretched before her. Hanna studied at the agricultural school of Nahalal, and then went to the settlement of Sedot Yam to live and work with other *Halutzim*. Hanna would have been happy had it not been for what was happening in Europe.

Even stronger than her desire to live in Palestine was her desire to return to Europe, to rescue as many Jews as she could from the Nazis.

So Hanna volunteered to become a parachutist, knowing that she might never return to the peaceful life of Sedot Yam. She was parachuted into Hungary, a young Jewish volunteer of twenty-three, dressed in the uniform of the British. There was little, however, that Hanna could do in Hungary, for she was soon caught by the Nazis and executed. But Hanna kindled a flame, and though Hanna died, the flame burned on.

Enzo Sereni was an Italian Jew, the son of the physician to the king of Italy. He too came to Palestine to work as a *Halutz*. In 1944, Enzo Sereni was dropped into Italy to work behind enemy lines. Like Hanna Senesch, Sereni was killed by the Nazis, who had occupied Italy. But the flame he kindled too burned on.

Not all the parachutists died at the hands of the Nazis. Avi, who had been a shepherd in Palestine, was dropped into Rumania, landed on a rooftop, broke his leg, and was captured. When his captors questioned him to find where he had come from and why he had come, Avi admitted only that he was a British lieutenant, and he insisted on being treated as a prisoner of war. After hours of torture, when his questioners could get nothing from him except that he was a British officer, he was removed to the hospital of the prison camp. From his hospital bed, with the help of a friendly nurse and a doctor, Avi was able to direct the escape of American and British prisoners of war, and to help hundreds of Jews escape from **Rumania**.

Joshua Trachtenburg, another parachutist, organized an underground railway. Using this railway, three thousand Jews escaped from Rumania and safely reached Palestine.

Thousands of Jews were saved because of the parachutists who were willing to die, so that they might kindle a flame.

Ma'apilim

Despite the small quota of Jews that Britain permitted to enter Palestine, thousands of Jews without certificates of entry managed to enter the land. They were not called immigrants, or refugees, by the Jews of Palestine. They were called *Ma'apilim*, which means, those who advance against great obstacles. Often they traveled for many months, from country to country, through underground railways and over mountains, till they reached Palestine at last.

"We Will Defend the Right"

England did not watch idly while the *Ma'apilim* entered Palestine. Her planes and cruisers and destroyers patrolled the waters of the Mediterranean Sea, on the lookout for little vessels bringing their human cargo to Palestine. Her soldiers searched the settlements, hunting for men and women without certificates.

Often the little vessels were caught, and the passengers were either sent back to Europe or held in detention camps. In the winter of 1941, the small vessel *Struma*, carrying more than seven hundred Jewish passengers, steamed into the port of Istanbul, in Turkey. But the Turkish authorities would not let the passengers pass through Turkey, because they had no certificates. The *Struma* remained in port for two months, her passengers aboard, waiting for Britain to give them certificates to enter Palestine. Finally, when the captain of the vessel realized that Britain would not issue certificates, he turned back to Europe. But once the boat left the neutral waters of Turkey, it was torpedoed and sunk, and only two passengers survived.

Many lives were lost, but many were saved through the heroism of the *Yishuv*. "We will defend the right of every Jew to enter the Jewish homeland!" became the slogan of the *Yishuv*. The *Haganah* chartered vessels to bring Jews to Palestine. When the vessels were expected, members of the *Haganah* were on hand to bring the *Ma'apilim* ashore. After the war they often blew up the

British radar and coastal guard stations to escape detection. Units of the *Haganah* would row out in boats, take on passengers, and bring them into port. Once on land, the *Ma'apilim* found a chain of *Haganah* soldiers to guard them as they were conducted to the inland settlements waiting to receive them.

The Hanna Senesch

A vessel called *Hanna Senesch,* named for the brave young parachutist who had died in Hungary, approached the coast of Naharya on a stormy night in the winter of 1945. Silently, the *Ma'apilim* aboard the *Hanna Senesch* lowered themselves into the rowboats that were to take them to shore. But so rough were the waves that the rowboats overturned in the waters. As the passengers floundered about, unable to swim to shore, members of the *Haganah,* stationed along the coastline, dove into the stormy sea. Each took a *Ma'apil* on his shoulder and swam back to shore. The *Hanna Senesch* drifted in toward the shoreline, and a human chain was formed from the vessel to the shore. All the remaining passengers were passed along from one man to another, till every *Ma'apil* was safely landed.

The next morning the British found the overturned vessel stranded on a sandbar. On the ship, soldiers of the *Haganah* had left a Jewish flag and a message which declared that they would continue to bring their people to Palestine.

After the War

The Second World War ended in 1945. The millions of Jews in Europe had been reduced to thousands. Many of those who survived had no homes to which they could return. Most of them wanted to go to Palestine. But the White Paper still kept the doors of Palestine closed.

As the *Yishuv* went on fighting the White Paper, the world watched in amazement. The tiny country with a population of thousands was defying the mighty world empire of Great Britain. And as the world watched a wonderful thing came to pass. Out of the struggle a nation was reborn. The name of the nation was Israel.

⋎⋎⋎ *For the Pupil*

THINGS TO READ:

Pessin, Deborah, *Giants on the Earth,* Part Two, "Exile," page 115, "A Sword Upon My Coffin," page 17.

THINGS TO TALK ABOUT:

1. Discuss the poem written by Hanna Senesch quoted in the chapter you have just read.
2. What problems did the *Yishuv* face in absorbing thousands of new settlers? What problems did the *Ma'apilim* face?

THINGS TO DO:

1. Write to the Zionist Organization of America for any material they have on the work of the *Yishuv* and *Haganah* during the Second World War.
2. Write the adventures of a *Ma'apil*.
3. Do a drawing or a painting showing the members of the *Haganah* rescuing the passengers of the *Hanna Senesch*.

Teacher's Bibliography

Berg, Mary, *Warsaw Diary*, L. B. Fischer, 1945.

Grayzel, Solomon, *A History of the Jews*, pp. 765-774; 782-795.

Hirschman, Ira, *Life Line to a Promised Land*, Jewish Book Guild of America, 1946.

Kressman, Taylor, *Address Unknown*, Schuster, New York, 1939.

Learsi, Rufus, *Israel*, pp. 650-664.

Syrkin, Marie, *Blessed Is the Match*, Jewish Publication Society, 1947.

Van Paasen, Pierre, *The Forgotten Ally*, Dial, 1943.

CHAPTER FOUR

Israel

The Partition Plan

When Great Britain realized that the situation in Palestine was more than she wanted to handle, she decided to bring the matter before the United Nations, which had taken the place of the League of Nations. The United Nations appointed a committee to investigate the problem. The members of the committee went to Palestine, where they could speak to Arabs and Jews and see for themselves what the situation was.

In September, 1947, the committee reported to the United Nations. It suggested that England give up the Mandate, and that Palestine be divided into two states, a Jewish state and an Arab state. Jerusalem, the committee suggested, should be internationalized and put under the control of the United Nations. England, however, was to keep the Mandate till the following year, and during that time, she was to maintain peace in Palestine.

The decision of the United Nations came two months later, on November 29, 1947. Palestine was to be divided into two states, an Arab and a Jewish state, with Jerusalem internationalized.

A wave of joy swept through the Jewish communities

UNITED NATIONS' PARTITION OF PALESTINE

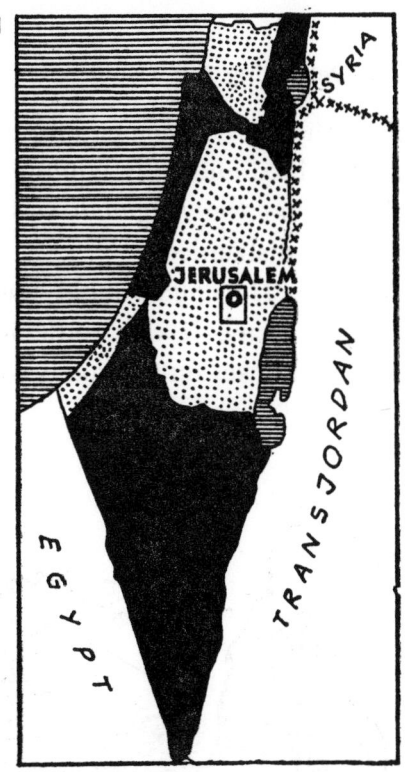

- ■ JEWISH
- ▦ ARAB
- □ INTERNATIONAL

of the world. In Palestine, the people danced in the streets and cheered and sang. The Partition Plan gave them less than half of tiny Palestine, but they were to be a nation again in their ancient homeland. With the approval of the United Nations, Israel was to have a homeland.

But even as the Jews celebrated the decision of the United Nations, Arab riots broke out again. From the neighboring states, from Egypt, Iraq, Arabia, Syria, Transjordan, Arab infiltration into Palestine began. The Arabs came into Palestine as "irregulars," armed for war.

Defending the Yishuv

Though the Arabs came into Palestine in the thousands, well-trained and fully equipped for war, the British declared that the *Haganah* was an illegal army, and ordered it disbanded.

So the *Haganah* fought underground to defend the land of Israel. Jewish settlements were attacked. Convoys and buses on the roads were fired on by Arab artil-

DEFENDING THE ROAD TO JERUSALEM

Israel

lery hidden in the hills. The road between Jerusalem and Tel-Aviv, the main road of communication to the Holy City, was under constant fire.

But neither the *Haganah* nor the general population weakened under the attacks. *Haganah* fighters searched the hills commanding Jerusalem, routing the Arab nests again and again. In Jerusalem, food and water were rationed. But the people went coolly about their daily tasks, taking hunger and thirst in their stride.

Invasion

When the fighting had gone on, month after month, the government of the United States decided that the Partition Plan would not work. It suggested, instead, that Palestine be put under a trusteeship of the United Nations.

The *Yishuv*, however, refused to consider a trusteeship. It had been promised independence, and it decided to win independence.

All the land was alerted for withstanding the Arab attacks. Men, women and children prepared to defend themselves against the invaders. The Jews did not have tanks, planes, or heavy artillery, as did the Arabs. But the Jews, said David ben Gurion, the head of the Jewish Agency, had a secret weapon, their spirit, their will to be free. Every Jew knew what he was fighting for—his freedom and the right to live in his own land.

The Proclamation

On Friday morning, May 14, 1948, the British Mandate for Palestine ended. On that day the British High Commissioner for Palestine boarded a vessel docked in the port of Haifa and sailed for home.

That afternoon, on May 14, 1948, David ben Gurion, the head of the Jewish Agency, read his people's proclamation of independence. In the midst of the fighting, the message of freedom sounded from every radio in the land.

". . . we, the members of the National Council, representing the Jewish people in Palestine and the Zionist movement of the world, met together in solemn assembly by virtue of the natural and historic right of the Jewish people and the resolution of the General Assembly of the United Nations, hereby

...אנו מכריזים בזאת על
הקמת מדינה יהודית בא"י.
היא מדינת ישראל.

proclaim the establishment of the Jewish state in Palestine, to be called Israel. . . ."

The United States of America, under President Harry Truman, was the first nation to recognize the new state of Israel. After the United States, other great powers recognized Israel, which had now taken its place in the family of nations.

Fighting for Independence

But peace did not come to the new state of Israel. The Arab leaders had threatened an invasion of Palestine once the British Mandate was ended. On the very day the British High Commissioner sailed for England and the proclamation was read, Arab troops swarmed into Israel from Egypt, Transjordan, Iraq, Syria, Lebanon. Some time later, troops from Saudi Arabia also joined the fight. The plan of the invaders was to conquer all of Palestine quickly and "drive the Jews into the sea."

But not all the might of the invaders, not all the artillery, planes, tanks, mortar and cannon were able to break the spirit of the new-born nation fighting for its life. Section after section of the Old City of Jerusalem passed into the hands of the Arabs. Finally, all of the Old City was taken. The attack on the New City of Jerusalem, with a population of ninety thousand, began. The road to Jerusalem was completely cut off, leaving the city with a serious shortage of food, water and electricity. But the defenders fought on. Under constant fire, the New City still buzzed with activity. And as the inhabitants of Jerusalem carried on, a new secret road was built over hills and

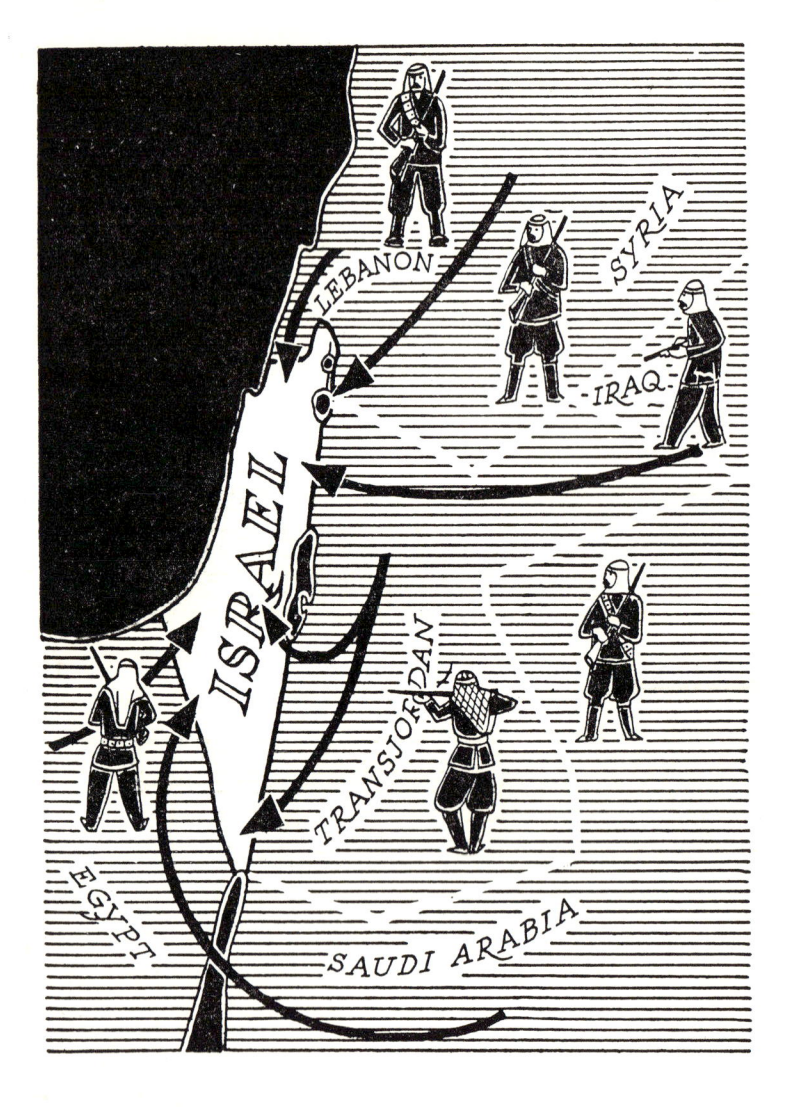

INVASION of ISRAEL by the ARAB STATES

☐ - ISRAEL   ▭ - ARAB STATES   ➤ DIRECTION OF ATTACK

precipices, by Jews outside Jerusalem. The road was built by thousands of men working at night by flashlight, so that they would not be spotted by the Arabs.

The fighting grew more intense. Settlement after settlement was attacked. But each attack was repelled. The attack against the settlement of Mishmar Ha-emek, carried out with heavy tanks and mortar and cannons, was repelled with only hand grenades. In the city of Haifa, in the city of Jaffa, in Jerusalem, in Safed, the Jews won each battle, despite the great odds against them.

The Arab agents, during all this time, kept up their work among the Arab peasants and city workers, telling them they would lose all they had under a Jewish state, filling them with fear of the *Haganah*. In Haifa, almost the whole Arab population fled at the approach of the *Haganah*, so terrified were they of the Jewish defenders. But there were many Arabs in Palestine by this time who refused to believe the tales of horror they were told. They had lived with the Jews for many years and they knew that they could live together in friendship.

The colony of Negba, in the south of Palestine, had been made a fertile spot in the wilderness of the Negev. The lonely colony was attacked by Egyptian Arabs using long range guns and planes. As the guns pounded away at Negba, planes circled overhead, dropping their loads of bombs. The buildings of Negba were finally destroyed, but its defenders, armed only with rifles and grenades, carried on from underground shelters. They never surrendered Negba, the oasis they had created in the hot wilderness in the south of Palestine.

CHAIM WEIZMANN
TAKING THE OATH OF OFFICE

In every settlement and city attacked by the Arabs, the same miracle took place. Heavy artillery and planes and tanks proved no match for the descendants of the Maccabees fighting for their independence. The tables were turned as the Arabs were driven out of Galilee, the

Israel

Negev, and from the wide corridor leading to Jerusalem. *Haganah* troops even invaded Lebanon and Egypt.

In January, 1949, an armistice was declared and the war was over. Although the Old City of Jerusalem, Gaza, and a portion of central Palestine remained in the hands of the Arabs, the State of Israel was considerably larger than what it had been under the partition plan.

In the same month that the war with the Arabs ended, in January, 1949, the new State of Israel held its first elections. Jews and Arabs went to the polls to elect their representatives to the Constituent Assembly. In February, the Constituent Assembly met and elected Dr. Chaim Weizmann president of Israel, while David ben Gurion was elected prime minister.

Several months later, in May, 1949, the State of Israel was admitted to the United Nations. After almost two thousand years the dream had come true. Israel was again a nation.

For the Pupil

THINGS TO TALK ABOUT:

1. Compare the fight of the *Yishuv* with the struggle of the Maccabees in ancient days.
2. Why did the Arab leaders wait for the British Mandate to end before beginning a full scale invasion of Palestine?
3. Discuss the proclamation of Israel, as quoted in your text book.

THINGS TO DO:

1. Pretend you were living in Jerusalem during the days of the Arab invasion. Write a diary describing what happened, to

you, to your family, friends. Describe the resistance of the city.
2. Make up a small newspaper issued on the day the Arabs invaded Palestine.

Teacher's Bibliography

Eisenberg, Azriel (Editor) *Modern Jewish Life in Literature*, Parts Three, Four and Five.

Grayzel, Solomon, *A History of the Jewish People*, pp. 795-800.

Learsi, Rufus, *Israel*, pp. 664-680.

Levin, Meyer, *My Father's House*, Viking Press, 1947.

Zeligs, Dorothy, *The Story of Modern Israel*, Bloch Publishing Co., 1950, Part Three, pp. 271-336.

DURING the long course of their history in the four corners of the world, the Jews acquired many different habits and customs. They wore the clothes, they spoke the languages of the people among whom they lived. Even the color of their skin often underwent change. But the heart of Jewish life remained the same, true to the ideals of Torah and the teachings of the prophets. In modern Israel as in America and in other lands, Jewish life and Jewish history continue.

INDEX

Abraham, 29
Abramovitch, Shalom Jacob, see Mendele Mokher Sefarim
Adams, John, 202
Africa, 19
Ahad Ha-Am, 185-187
Ahavat Tziyon, 164
Alexander I, 150-152
Alexander II, 158, 160-161, 166
Alexander III, 166, 167
Aliyah, 185, 261, 262, 264
Allenby, General, 267
Alliance Israélite Universelle, 173
Altneuland, 183, 184
Amalgamated Clothing Workers of America, 243
America, 14, 16, 57, 118, 127, 169, 191-255
American Jewish Committee, 250, 253
American Revolution, 118, 201, 203
Amsterdam, 39, 42, 43, 47, 48
Antiochus, 12
Antwerp, 23
Arabia, 260, 272
Arabs, 259
Argentina, 180
ARI, see Luria
Asia, 20
Assyria, 12
Astrakhan, 150, 151

Austria, 102, 148
Auto-Emancipation, 174

Baal Shem Tov, 97, 99-105
Babylonia, 12
Baḥur, 79, 85-87, 162-164
Balfour Declaration, 266-267, 270
Basle, 182
Ben Gurion, David, 297, 298, 303
Ben Yehudah, Eliezer, 276-277
Bene Yeshurun, 218
Berlin, 120
Beth Joseph, 37
Bible, 33, 52, 201
Bill of Rights, 204
BILU, 175, 261
Bnai Brith, 212
Bohemia, 216
Bolsheviks, 249-250
Book of Ben Sirah, 222-223
Book of Psalms, 124
Brazil, 54, 55, 57, 191, 192
Bremen, 128
Brest, 73
British Guiana, 56
British Mandate for Palestine, 273, 294, 297, 299
Brown, John, 214
Budapest, 178
Bulgaria, 171, 181

Cairo, 34, 35, 93, 224
Cantonists, 153-155
Carpathian Mountains, 99
Catherine II, Czarina of Russia, 149
Caucasus, 150, 151
Central Conference of American Rabbis, 220
Charleston, 201
Chmelnitzki, 90-91
Cincinnati, 218, 219
Civil War, 213-214
Cologne, 129
Columbus, 11, 16, 52
Conservative Judaism, 139-140, 220-222
Constantinople, 23
Constituent Assembly, 303
Copernicus, 51
Cossacks, 89-91
Council of the Four Lands, see Va'ad Arba Aratzot
Cracow, 71, 78
Crimea, 90
Cromwell, Oliver, 45-46
Crown Schools, 155-157
Crusaders, 26
Cyrus, 12, 267

Daniel Deronda, 173
David, 29
Dayanim, 62, 75
Dead Sea, 275
Deborah, 219
Declaration of Independence, 204
Dessau, 120, 122

Dreyfus, Alfred, 178, 179
Dutch, 54-55, 192, 193
Dutch West Indies Company, 54, 193

Easton, 201
Ecclesiasticus, see Book of Ben Sirah
Egypt, 20, 34, 35, 224, 260, 265, 272, 299, 303
Einhorn, Dr. David, 213
Elhanan, Rabbi Isaac, 229
Elijah, 35
Elijah, Gaon, 107-111
Eliot, George, 172, 173
Elizabeth, Czarina of Russia, 147
Emancipation, 119, 132
England, 18, 45-46, 51, 191, 200, 265-266
Enlightenment, 161-162
Eretz Yisrael, see Palestine
Essen Teg, 85
Ethics, 49

Feast of Weeks, see Shavuot
Federation, 245
Ferdinand, 14, 21
First World War, 248-249, 261
Fraenkel, Rabbi David, 121
France, 18, 51, 119, 127-129, 191
Frankel, Zechariah, 139-140
Frankfort, 129
Franklin, Benjamin, 202
French Revolution, 127-129, 132

INDEX

Galicia, 70
Galilee, 29, 35, 302
Galileo, 51
Gaza, 303
Geiger, Abraham, 139
Genizah, 223-225
Georgia, 197
Germanic Lands, 14, 18, 54, 64, 65, 78, 79, 115-144, 207, 212-213
Germany, 51, 67, 102, 171
Ghetto, 115-117, 128
Ginzberg, Asher, see Ahad Ha-Am
Gordon, Judah Leib, 162, 164
Graetz, Heinrich, 142-143
Great Poland, 70

Hadassah, 264-265
Haganah, 274-275, 290, 296-297, 301, 303
Haifa, 270-271, 301
Halutzim, 262
Hamburg, 136
Ha-Me'assef, 124
Hanna Senesch, 291-292
Ha-Shaḥar, 172
Ha-Shiloah, 187
Ḥasidim, 102, 103-107
Ḥasidism, 102-107
Haskalah, 161-166
Havlagah, 275
Hebrew Union College, 220
Hebrew University, 267, 270
Hebron, 29
Ḥeder, 79-82, 117, 243

Heidelberg, University of, 48
Herzl, Theodor, 176, 178-184
Hess, Moses, 171, 172, 174, 179
Hessians, 204
Hirsch, Baron de, 180
Hirsch, Rabbi Samson Raphael, 137-138
Histadrut Haovdim, 264
Historical Judaism, see Conservative Judaism
Hitler, 277-278
Holland, 14, 39-48, 51, 54, 56, 128, 191, 192, 193
Holy Cities, 29
Hovevei Tziyon, 173, 175, 180
Hungary, 54, 181, 287, 288

India, 26
Indians, 45, 53, 201
Inquisition, 14, 19, 41, 45, 53, 54
International Ladies Garment Workers Union, 243
Iraq, 260, 272, 299
Isaac, 29
Isabella, 14
Isaiah, 175
Israel, 12, 14, 259-303
Israelite, 219
Isserles, Moses, 117
Italy, 19, 51, 128, 288

Jacob, 29
Jacobson, Israel, 136
Jaffa, 185, 270, 301
Jaroslaw, 76